D0937342

GROUP LEADERSHIP

A MANUAL FOR GROUP COUNSELING LEADERS

Marilyn M. Bates
Department of Behavioral Sciences
California State College, Fullerton

Clarence D. Johnson
Department of Behavioral Sciences
California State College, Fullerton

LOVE PUBLISHING COMPANY DENVER, COLORADO 80222

EDUCATION SERIES

Copyright © 1972 Love Publishing Company
All rights reserved
Printed in the U. S. A.
Library of Congress Catalogue Card Number 70-177987

Second Printing, 1973

CONTENTS

PREFACE

If the assumption is correct that experience as a group member is a necessary *and sufficient* preparation for group leadership, this book need not be. If the assumption is correct that being a group member equips a group leader with the intellectual and experiential tools required to run a group, this book need not be. The authors believe that both the above assumptions are incorrect, misleading, and antithetical to responsible group leadership.

It is the position of the writers that, while group membership is a necessary preparation for group leadership, it is *not* sufficient in itself. We believe that the experience of group membership is essentially different from the experience of group leadership because the former requires an intense focusing on self, while the latter requires an intense loosening—almost abnegation—of self. The group member looks inward and relates outward; the group leader looks outward and relates inward. The cognitive and emotional processes inherent in the two roles are quite different from each other, and while we believe that being a member is essential preparation for being a leader, we also see it as only that—preparatory.

Further, it is our firm conviction that group leadership can and must be taught. The group leader must have the professional tools which will enable him to activate group processes in a way which insures that members have growth-producing experiences. The main focus of this book is to present such tools. The theoretical constructs which provide the rationale from which the tools are derived are termed "The Extensional Group Model."

The material presented in this publication is directed toward the leader who leads self-actualizing groups. The paradigm presented is a "well" model rather than a "remedial" model; consequently it is appropriate for leaders who work within institutional settings (public schools, probation departments, etc.) as well as for those who work outside institutional settings (marriage counseling groups, family counseling groups, etc.) .

Marilyn Bates
C. D. Johnson

CHAPTER 1

THE EXTENSIONAL GROUP MODEL: A MODERN PHILOSOPHICAL AND THEORETICAL FRAMEWORK

To the Group Leader:

The Extensional Group provides the model of this book for Group Leaders. It may provide a model for you as you lead groups.

CHAPTER 1

THE EXTENSIONAL GROUP MODEL: A MODERN PHILOSOPHICAL AND THEORETICAL FRAMEWORK

Groups can be for better or for worse. While it is inconceivable that a leader deliberately sets out to form a group for worse, the literature from all disciplines dealing with interaction groups is beginning to reflect that many group experiences do diminish or almost destroy their members (Eddy & Lubin, 1971; Howard, 1970; Shostrom, 1970; Yalom, 1971). Participants may approach interaction groups anticipating one type of experience and find something quite different. As a result of proliferating reports of "for worse" group experiences, more and more professionals and more and more of the lay public are becoming skeptical of interaction groups (Goldberg, 1970). A high probability exists that many people who could use group processes for positive growth avoid getting involved for fear of a destructive experience. Yet groups *can* be for better. In the hands of an adequately trained leader participants need not fear a destructive experience, but can anticipate positive growth. Competent leaders provide this insurance.

Training group leaders to handle group processes so that members have a positive experience is the focus of this book. Such training involves both theory and practice. Part One presents the philosophical and theoretical framework of the model; Part Two presents the practice derived from the philosophy and theory.

The group model which provides the conceptual framework for this manual is termed the "Extensional Group." The Extensional Group which is based on a well model is contrasted in the following pages with a Remedial Group model. The philosophical foundation of the Extensional Group—Existentialism—is presented by describing selected concepts of this philosophy as they apply to the Extensional Group model.

Group Leadership

The Remedial and Extensional Group Models are presented in order to delineate clearly two interaction experiences which differ both in purpose and in process and to delineate clearly the theoretical stance of the authors of this book. The Remedial Group is mainly a therapy group which is based on a medical model and is primarily motivated from deficiency needs of members. The Extensional Group is seen as a self-actualizing group which is based on a developmental conceptualization and is motivated primarily by the growth needs of members.

REMEDIAL GROUPS

Much confusion seems to exist concerning groups which may be formed for what is essentially the remediation of inadequate personal functioning and groups which may be formed for *extending adequate personality functioning.* "Ill" people need to get better. Well people also can get better. Remedial groups are concerned with the former— ill persons who are not currently coping with the stresses and strains of living. The group leader conducting a remedial group may find that members must regress before they can mobilize their positive growth forces. Members may need to "act out" their hostilities in infantile fashion before they can release non-hostile forces. They may need to vent angers, fears, and hates exhaustively before they are able to express love, caring, and hope. This type of group does, indeed, need to "work through" much negative content before positive content can surface.

The mistake many group leaders have made is to assume that *all* groups must regress to more primitive forms of behavior before growth forces can be activated. Traditionally, leaders have assumed that *all* members must discharge energies cathected toward experiences charged with hate, fear, and anger. The initial group sessions, then, were necessarily directed toward eliciting expressions of irrational, id-based, infantile behaviors. Once this cycle was completed, members could move on to explore new ways of behaving which were more mature, rational, and ego-based.

That regression is necessary and appropriate in a remedial group is recognized. Groups composed of members who need to repair personality defects must scrape off layers of debilitating defense

10

mechanisms before the core of personality can be restructured even minimally. Leaders of remedial, regressive groups require training in the medical model: the psychiatrist, the psychotherapist, the clinical psychologist.

THE EXTENSIONAL GROUP

The traditional stance that groups are primarily for ill people and that a regressive, acting-out, remedial process must take place initially in *all* groups is outmoded. The point of view of this book is that groups *can* serve another function—extending life space of members by extending the capabilities of even those members who may currently be functioning at a satisfactory or even a self-actualizing level of existence. This particular use of groups has been confused with the remedial use of groups. That a differentiation of procedures is mandated for the two types has not been clear. This chapter specifies differences in assumptions and procedures between a remedial group and an extensional group.

The Extensional group model which is applicable to both students and nonstudents begins with the assumption that well people can get *better* and group is one arena where this can occur. The Extensional group focuses on the concept that even people who are functioning adequately, who are fairly comfortable in interpersonal relationships, who may be coping with the demands of daily living, can still experience growth in a self-actualizing paradigm. Members of this type of group are "well" rather than "ill" but want to get better, i.e., want to free learning ability; want to attain more enjoyment from living; want more spontaneity, more creativity, more autonomy, more acceptance of necessary restrictions, more joy, more productivity, more awareness and acceptance of themselves and of others —in short, want to accelerate the process of self-actualization. The Extensional group provides an opportunity for members to explore more satisfying ways of behaving in relation to self and in relation to one another. The existent life-space of each member can be examined thoroughly without threat of this life-space being diminished. The existent life-spaces of members as they interface can also be explored without fear of negation.

The Extensional group model anticipates that members leave each session and the group experience itself augmented rather than diminished. Through the group experience each member extends facets of his personality and strengths in growth directions. This model is developmental rather than remedial, and extensional rather than regressive. The leader, then, does not assume that negative forces must be siphoned off before positive forces can be manifest. He can begin at the growth stations of members and move on rather than, as in the Remedial group, encourage members to regress to earlier forms of behavior with the intent of working through or minimizing blocks to development. Each member can begin with the base "I'm okay, you're okay" (Harris, 1969), and proceed to develop specifics to elaborate that stance.

The Poles

The Remedial group is conceptualized as operating mainly on a

FIGURE 1-1

TWO GROUP MODELS

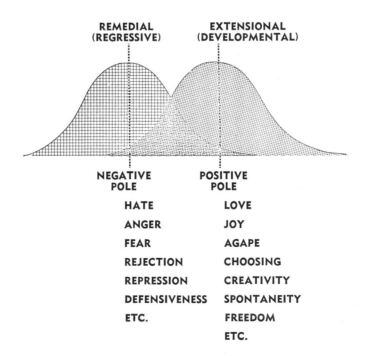

REMEDIAL (REGRESSIVE)	EXTENSIONAL (DEVELOPMENTAL)
NEGATIVE POLE	**POSITIVE POLE**
HATE	LOVE
ANGER	JOY
FEAR	AGAPE
REJECTION	CHOOSING
REPRESSION	CREATIVITY
DEFENSIVENESS	SPONTANEITY
ETC.	FREEDOM
	ETC.

negative pole, *i.e.*, dealing with negative content such as hate relationships, anger toward authority figures, resentment of early experiences, debilitating defense mechanisms—in general, behaviors which are primarily based in a more primitive ego state. The group leader needs to be prepared to deal with many negative forces in the Remedial group, and he will find that one negative comment tends to generate others. The negative elements in the group cause others to emerge, which in turn will trigger additional negative interaction. Thus, the initial content of the group interaction may focus on potentially destructive elements.

In the Extensional group, leaders will be dealing primarily with positive forces and will find that one positive force tends to generate another. The positive elements in these groups will incubate others, and a reinforcing cycle is activated.

The two types of groups described overlap to some degree; hence, the Remedial group will process positive forces, just as the Extensional group will deal with a proportion of negative content. Figure 1 provides a diagram of these two types of groups. It will be noted that where the Remedial group and the Extensional group overlap, the former contains positive content, while the latter gains negative content. The diagram serves to illustrate the proportionate amount of negative or positive content which is likely to exist initially in either type of group.

PHILOSOPHICAL BASE OF THE EXTENSIONAL GROUP

The philosophical foundation of the Extensional group is in the Existentialist framework. The authors of this book have discussed the implications of Existentialism for the individual counseling relationship elsewhere (Bates and Johnson, 1969) and propose in the following pages to specify the implications of an Existentialist stance for leaders of Extensional groups.

The massive proliferation of "groups" represents a current phenomenon. Alienation, loss of purpose, impersonalization, dehumanization, all seem part of the *Zeitgeist* of our times. If it is true that a particular philosophy reflects the *Zeitgeist* of each age, the philosophy of Existentialism most certainly reflects the anguish of mid-century man as he despairs of "Truth" in a shattered world. The search for meaning, for encounter, for I-Thou, the confirmation of a universal *angst* as a basic condition of man, the facing of the loneliness of responsible choices—all these thread contemporary thought as familiar ideas which have profound implications for the leader of an Extensional group.

Many people perceive the philosophy termed "Existentialism" as obscure and Godless, redundant and solipsistic, reactionary and anti-Establishment. Others who have struggled with the convolutions of Existentialist thought have found ideas which have been lucid, spiritual, challenging, and comforting. Internalizing the concepts of this philosophy often has been, for those who persevere, a very intense and personal experience. Group leaders who work from within an Existentialist framework find that leading a group is a very intense, personal experience.

The concepts of Existentialism relevant to group processes are articulated in the first person since they are very personal statements. The implications for leaders of Extensional Groups are delineated next. Illustrative dialogues are provided where appropriate.

EXISTENTIALIST CONCEPT: EXISTENCE PRECEDES ESSENCE

A World Without Givens. I find myself thrown into a world void of all prior meaning. I find that I have arrived on the scene of life without a road map of the territory. I know one and only one certainty—death. Nothing else from this time on is a "given." No script has been written which I can consult. I am given no models, no "grand designs," no assurance that there is a teleological carpet which unfolds as I move toward death. I am on my own—alone. I know that I exist. Now I must define myself and try to make meaning out of this world without meaning. I am completely free because there is no *a priori*. I am faced with the task of creating my world which offers limitless possibilities without pre-established requirements. I exist. I find myself free to define my essence and however I choose to define myself is up to me. I know that my statement concerning my essence will be unique just as every man's is unique. I know that I am different from any human being who ever lived before me or who ever will live after me and I conceive of myself as fluid rather than static, moving rather than still, evolving rather than evolved, never finished.

My Signature of Essence. So I find that I am my own essence-giver. My life is an unanswered question to be answered however I choose. There are many times when I cry for the security of someone who will define me in the morass of this dreadful ambiguity where all the certainty I have available is that at the end of my defining, death awaits. I know that I will be flung back into

14

another unknown, perhaps like the unknown from which I was flung, but this time the unknown is ahead of me, an anticipation rather than a residual memory and—a certainty. Between this terrible nothing and nothing I must make a statement concerning my essence. I am filled with *angst* because of the unknowns which dwell on either side of me. I cry for the security of "givens." I do not like being on my own, alone, undefined, forced to choose whatever I will. I feel a terrible nausea for life welling up in me. I would like to escape by default, to choose not to choose, but then this becomes a choice and I meet myself face to face, filled with *angst* and despair.

My Primal and My Subsequent Choices. Out of my *angst* and nausea with life I must make a primal choice. I must choose to live or to die. Since for the moment I decide to live, I will live my life in such a way so as to deserve something better than nothingness. I will use my becoming so as to deny the futility of existence and try to make my life a statement which ought never to be obliterated even though I know that in the end it will be. Since essence is up to me, perhaps I can be worthy of existing and undeserving of being lost to the universe. I will try to have the courage to be. I will try to use my encounter with nothingness to affirm myself. I will try to have the courage to demonstrate my worth to a world in which my existence is not in question. I know that I exist, but I am aware that my *essence* is in question and I want my essence to be worthy of existing forever.

IMPLICATIONS FOR AN EXTENSIONAL GROUP OF THE EXISTENTIAL CONCEPT: EXISTENCE PRECEDES ESSENCE

The group member as well as the leader is faced with the task of defining his essence. This concept is fundamental to the Existential view of the nature of man. A group cannot define essence for its members, who all share the human state of being thrown from oblivion into an ambiguous world. It does not follow, however, that interaction is an empty ritual without meaning. At first glance it would seem that this was the case, for if each man must define himself, what possible use could be made of group processes? If defining essence is an individual task, what place is there for the group relationship?

The answer lies in man's essential loneliness. Each man is alone, but is not aware of his loneliness until he interfaces with another human being. Then and only then is he aware of his essential state of isolation. If man were dropped newborn on an unpopulated isle, and by some miracle survived physically, he would not become human in the Existentialist sense. He could not define himself without coming into contact with other humans. It is only by interacting with another that he becomes aware he exists. It is only through this interface that he can define himself. Group provides a rare and valuable opportunity to experience one's self through interacting with trained leaders and with other members. Man's need to define essence begs for opportunities to work with others, and a group experience can provide an unparalleled arena for this purpose. The essential, human lifelong task of defining essence is the most important process in which man will be involved, and it should not be left to casual relationships only. Man exists. He must define his essence. Group is one place to record signatures and to clarify existences.

A representative multilogue might clarify the concept of man's loneliness being shared in a group:

Joan: "I feel uneasy when I walk into a room full of people. I don't know what to do, or say, or really, to be. . . ."

Lillie: "Yeah, that's how I am. I get tight inside, kind of queasy and don't know what to do, especially with my hands."

Leader: "Right now I'm experiencing the same feelings. Kind of tight, and sort of separate from you, and yet knowing you are here makes me feel stronger."

The Essence of the Group Leader

A group experience cannot change each member's essential sentence of having to define himself, but it can midwife the process of becoming. Group members and leaders can walk together as each struggles with his essence. The group can share the pain of the constant metamorphosis which is becoming, and by sharing can be catalytic to the process. This sharing, however, holds special implications for the essence of the leaders. If leaders are destructive beings, a member can be hurt. If leaders are inauthentic, a member can be hurt. If the leaders are unskilled, a member can be hurt. There is mounting evidence in the literature that counseling can be harmful. The naive and comforting assumption that at worst counseling might be ineffective is no longer tenable. Apparently counselees who come in contact with counselors who are in poor psychological shape may leave the counseling relationship damaged (Carkhuff and Berenson, 1967). The responsibility of the profession to insure that this does

16

not happen is obvious, as are the implications for the selection and training of group leaders.

An example of a group leader being destructive might be:

Joan:	"I've tried and tried to stand up to my boss, but I just can't do it. I just turn into a child every time he is around."
Destructive Leader:	"You just have to be stronger. You aren't a little girl, you know, so why let him dominate you? Tell him off—tell him to go to hell—threaten to quit."

The Existentialist concept of "Existence Precedes Essence" involves counseling for leaders. Since a leader as well as a member is himself in process of becoming, leaders will need some source of what Carkhuff and Berenson (1967) term "human nourishment." The most elegant and harmonious choice for nourishment would be continuous, lifelong counseling for the leader, both individual and group. Leading a group is stimulating, but demanding. A leader who does not have a group in which he is a member may find himself using the groups he leads for his own needs, to the detriment of his group members. Who counsels the counselor is a relevant question for group leaders. A group where a leader can participate as member, where he can maintain his own growth toward self-actualization, a "maintenance group" for group leaders, seems essential as a way of professional life for those who lead groups.

The Choosing of Choices in an Extensional Group

The concept "Existence Precedes Essence" with its sentence of freedom leaves man living an unanswered question. He must make choices and live by these choices. Since man must choose, his best chance of being human is to make as many choices as possible in awareness. The Existentialist struggles constantly to maintain awareness of his freedom by trying to view every word and every act as an active choice, and hence, an act of value creation.

One of the Extensional group leader's tasks is to help each member bring into awareness his own freedom, which involves making choices in no awareness, in dim awareness, or in full awareness. Each participant through group processes can clarify alternatives open to him and can increase his sensitivity toward aware choices. A group leader can help a member think through contradictions, ambiguities, value goals, and fantasies which may be action-inhibiting and which may have blocked growth.

A leader also can help members examine consequences of alternatives. Members can be assisted to think through to logical conclusion various plans of action, and in so doing become aware of freedom. Each member also can examine the responsibility he carries for his chosen alternatives and face fully that he has no one on whom to shift this responsibility—neither counselor nor friend, teacher or parent. He and he alone must accept the consequences of his actions. He also must recognize that others will be affected by his actions and choices and he must bring into awareness the effect of his choices on others, for this represents part of his responsibility. Leaders must not overtly or covertly try to take away each member's responsibility in and out of group. Leaders are responsible for the group process, *not* for members. If a member chooses to be late, that is his choice; the leader begins on time. If a member chooses not to enter into the interaction, that is his choice; the leader creates the climate where interaction is available.

A dialogue to illustrate the clarification of alternatives might be:

Jim: "I can't get a job unless I cut my hair, but I think it looks creepy short. . . ."

Jane: "You must not need a job very bad then."

Leader: "At the moment you seem pulled two ways. . . ."

Jim: "I really am. I do need the job."

Sue: "You could buy a wig and push your hair up under it when you go look for a job."

Jim: "If I don't have a job, I don't have any money to buy a wig, do I? Besides, I'd feel stupid in a wig. I suppose I could cut my hair some. . . ."

18

Leader: "Of the ideas you have, having your hair at least somewhat shorter seems one alternative to consider."

A dialogue to illustrate the responsibility for choices may be useful:

Harry: "I'm a listener. I want to be sure of what I say before I talk."

Al: "I think you're taking a free ride, Harry. You take from the group but you don't give anything back."

Leader: "I relate to your choosing to talk on your own terms, Harry, but Al, I also relate to your reaction. I see you, Harry, as not willing to carry your share of group responsibility and this annoys me."

EXISTENTIALIST CONCEPT: MAN IS CONDEMNED TO FREEDOM

The Existentialist Paradox. I am free. No matter how much I would like to deny this awe-ful fact, I cannot. I am free—and this freedom contains a paradox. Because of my freedom the pronoun "I" has absolute priority in my existence. I am the only one of my kind and I cannot be classified. Since I am a singular phenomenon, I never will be repeated. I ought to be worthy of attention in the world. I can understand Morris's comment, "I am permanent, a datum written with indelible ink into the cosmic ledger book, never to be erased or expunged. I may be in very small print, but I am there forever. I assign to myself, therefore . . . an absolute value and an ultimate worth" (Morris, 1966: 16). Because I exist and I am I, the world would not be quite the same without me. This is one side of the Existentialist paradox.

The other side of the paradox which I hold in awareness is that my existence is a great delusion, a huge joke, because, as I think of the magnitude of the universe, I know that I count for absolutely nothing. The universe is indifferent to my presence. When I die, there may be a moment of stirring, but then nothing. Sooner than later my absence will be forgotten and, eventually, all traces of me will be erased from the universe. I try not to think of this inevitability too much because it brings on nausea and *angst*, but always I am haunted by awareness that my existence is completely irrelevant.

This is the paradox with which I live. To matter and not to matter. To be of absolute value in the world and to be of absolutely no value. These two truths are contradictory, but both are true. My subjectivity asserts the absoluteness of my value and my reason asserts the veracity of my valuelessness. These two facts are paradoxical, but I believe them both as an inescapable fact of my being condemned to freedom.

My Absolute Freedom: I Am My Values. The thought of my absolute freedom makes me angry. I do not wish to be free, to choose for myself, to be condemned to making choices "on my own." Surely there is someone or something who will direct me and eliminate the boundlessness of my responsibility. As it is, I must stand witness for all my statements as to who I am. I have total personal answerability for my involvement in life.

It is dread indeed to be free and aware of my freedom. The responsibility for all my choices carries an added burden. As I make my choices I create my value system. There is no one I can scapegoat, or blame, or burden with guilt. I would prefer an easier life, but I am free and am aware of my freedom. I am the sole author of my life and I must answer for all I do. The statement that I make about myself is that I am ready to respond to each moment with authentic responsibility and am ready to speak for my performance.

This authenticity towards which I strive is illusive. I try to be honest inwardly and outwardly, but I am subject to error. At any given moment of being I seem to myself to be authentic, but in backward glances I often find that my thoughts and behaviors were inconsistent with what I was really experiencing. I find that I cannot be wholly authentic, and this failure is a source of *angst* in me. I suffer pain because of anxiety and guilt generated by these failures. Intellectually I know that these failures are inevitable and a part of my human condition, but emotionally I react with a sense of incompleteness, a sense of never being total, a sense of freedom which is a burden rather than an inspiration.

There are rare moments when I transcend this sense of failure. At these times I am aware of moving forward, and I have a feeling of power over myself. In these instances I belong completely to myself and am in complete harmony with myself. I have the courage to be in full awareness and I expect that in these moments I am truly authentic. At other times I can only use my sentence of freedom to strive toward authenticity, and bear with what courage I can the *angst* which comes from failure. This is the inevitable tax levied with freedom, a price tagged to my condemnation.

IMPLICATIONS OF THE EXISTENTIAL CONCEPT: MAN IS CONDEMNED TO FREEDOM

The Existentialist Paradox and Human Nourishment

The paradoxical nature of man's freedom—to be of ultimate, absolute value and to be of absolutely no value—finds man in a condition of *angst* and nausea. He brings this *angst* and nausea to groups. The Extensional group offers an antidote—human nourishment.

The concept of human nourishment applies especially to the Extensional group. The notion that just as we need adequate physical nourishment daily in order to sustain good somatic health, so do we require daily human nourishment in order to sustain good psychological health, is particularly relevant to the idea of group as a vehicle for optimum personality development. In a regressive, remedial group the concept of the group process functioning as a purgative or cathartic would be an apt parallel to the concept of human nourishment in an Extensional group. It would be hoped that a remedial group would eventually begin to supply the basic minimum requirements of psychological food to its members until they were able to develop to the point where they could obtain it from their life-spaces outside the group. The Extensional group provides this automatically as members seek to extend themselves in self-actualization. "Human nourishment" is a spinoff of the Extensional group, but one which the leader can help members recognize as a basic need and which may be sought actively in life outside the group. At present there seem to be no units for measuring the amounts of human nourishment taken in or given, although Berne's (1961) "strokes" might be one reference point.

It seems logical to assume that people who are in good psychological health themselves can give more human nourishment than can people who are operating at a lower level of functioning. The implications for this thought are profound for the group process. If, as Carkhuff and Berenson (1968) maintain, individual counseling can be for better or for worse, it is almost certainly true also that a group can be for better or for worse. Consequently, if a member is misplaced in a remedial group, he may find that he gives nourishment but receives none in return and leaves the group badly diminished. In an Extensional group the human nourishment available should be abundant and no one need leave the group psychologically hungry.

A dialogue illustrating transmission of nourishment in a group multilogue follows:

Don: "I come to school in the morning and I just go to class day after day and I don't have any friends and I wonder what's wrong with me."

Cal: "I know what you mean. The only time I get to be with anyone is lunch time or when I talk on the phone at night."

Leo: "I'm glad to know that you both feel the way I do. I

21

     thought I was the only one who didn't seem to have
     friends and who was alone all the time."

Leader: "It seems to me that you are telling me that each of you
     is lonely and that you also feel better knowing that some-
     one else is in the same boat, that there are others who
     feel the same way you do."

Existential Freedom and Question of Values

The Existentialist group leader conceptualizes man as condemned
to a freedom from which there is no escape. It is the degree of awareness of that freedom which differentiates the Existentialist from the
non-Existentialist. The former, having become aware of the implications of his freedom, must stand up to it as best he can. The non-
Existentialist can enjoy the security of being other-directed.

At first glance the concept of freedom seems to pose problems for
the Extensional group leader, for the question of values is involved.
Does the leader have the right to impose his values on a member?

Existentialism deals with this concern rather easily, for in this
theoretical framework the question is irrelevant. Not only does the
leader have no right to impose his values, he *cannot,* for each man is
condemned to his own freedoms and must determine his own values.
To raise the question of forcibly or subtly imposed values is a contra-
diction of the Existentialist's concept of man as condemned to a
freedom from which there is no escape. This condition holds whether
or not man is aware of his freedom; group leaders are condemned to
freedom as are group members.

The preceding notion in no way implies that the leader is not his
value system. He *is,* and his values are transmitted full-force through
his behaviors, but he does not and cannot impose his values on others.
As the leader is available to members, so is his value system available.
Without this congruency, the leader could not be authentic. The leader of an Extensional group transmits to the group his feeling, reactions, his essence. He is always aware, however, that his function as
leader is to midwife the growth of group members, not to use the
group for his own needs. As the leader of an Extensional group interacts, he is acutely aware that his sharing of his authentic self is for the
use of the group. The leader is known, he is available, he is trans-

parent, but he does not give advice or manipulate members. When he reacts and interacts he does so to extend the life-space of members. The fact that his own life-space is expanded in the process is secondary to the primary purpose of his being there—to be of use to the group.

An example of the dialogue which reflects translation of this concept into action might be:

Cal: "I wish I could be honest with people but they wouldn't understand if I told them the truth—"

Leader: "I guess where I'm at is that if I weren't honest with you right now and say I withdraw from what you're saying with almost a physical repugnance, I would close out real communication between us."

In this dialogue the leader is stating clearly his existent reactions—not for his needs (which might be to contradict, to be "better than," etc.) but to make his essence available to the member who can use this content to hear what he really is saying, i.e., "I'm afraid I'll be rejected if I'm authentic, I prefer deceit, etc."

EXISTENTIALIST CONCEPT: MAN HIMSELF THROUGH HIS ACTIONS AND ONLY THROUGH HIS ACTIONS

I am condemned by my human state to make free choices, and I know no reprieve from responsibility for those choices. On each choice I stake my future and I am in a perpetual situation of crisis because I never am sure of the correctness of my choices. I also know that the way I define my essence is through my acts. I am continually emergent in my actions.

"What," not "Why." I wish I could verbalize good intentions and get credits on the "books." I wish that I could get credit for planning behavior and have it count, even though I never translated those plans into actions. But I know that my plans, my good intentions, my regrets, my whys are irrelevant until translated into action. Verbalizing a commitment to change is not action. What I actually do is my essence, my self-definition. Kierkegaard (1944) taught me this: that truth exists for a particular individual only as he himself produces it in action.

Thus I must act before I count.

The "Here and Now." I do not restrict my conceptualization of action to overt acts, but conceive my attitudes as part of the fabric of my actions. If I perform an act with reluctance, my reluctance defines some of that act. Everything which makes up my "I-ness" is relevant to my actions. The important idea of "I" is what I am *en toto,* and what I am now, this moment, here—not what I intend to be tomorrow, or what I intend to do tomorrow, or what I was yesterday, or what I did yesterday. Which means that I must stand in present tense with complete accountability for what I am today, concerned about my past actions only as they are relevant for the present, and concerned about my future actions only as they are relevant for the present.

IMPLICATIONS FOR AN EXTENSIONAL GROUP OF THE EXISTENTIAL CONCEPT: MAN DEFINES HIMSELF THROUGH HIS ACTIONS

"Why" versus "What" Counseling. The Extensional group leader who subscribes to the defining-through-action concept will never ask "Why?" of a group member; this would be considered irrelevant. Rather, focus of group exploration would be on "What." For example, a member who came to group with a conflict situation would not be faced with a futile cross-examination of being asked to explain the causes of his behavior but would report the What of the circumstances. What were his behaviors and what does he see as alternatives to action? And since the member is only in charge of himself and his actions, obviously any suggestion for solutions which require a change of behavior by another person, e.g., a teacher, would not be seen as consistent with the concept of each person being responsible for defining himself.

In a public school Extensional group, this emphasis on "What" behavior of a member permits the Existentialist leader to avoid the pitfall of defending a colleague. Since focus is on actions of the participant little attention is given to actions of a teacher or other persons concerned. This may distress a counselee who is accustomed to using a counselor as a sympathetic sounding board against whom to itemize the sins of others. The insistence of the Existentialist counselor on the counselee's talking about his own behaviors may at first be annoying, but as a counselee grows in self-respect and self-acceptance, the increasing awareness of responsibility will be refreshing. Perhaps one of the reasons that counseling, both individual and group, is seen so often as being of little value by students is that the group and individual session has been allowed to deteriorate into a self-pitying experience. The emphasis on "What" counseling, consistent with the concept of defining oneself through action, should

24

prove far more productive to counselee and counselor alike.

Illustrative dialogue:

Mary: "I try and try to be on time, but somehow I'm always late."

Leader: "It seems to me that the thing you *do* is be late. The thing you *intend* to do is be on time."

The Here and Now. The Existential concept of existence being in the here and now implies for the group leader that content will focus mainly on the here-and-now process within the group. The fluid relating of one member to another provides the material of group exploration. As one member reacts to another, he will be encouraged to verbalize this reaction. The current experiencing of each group member will be the subject matter of each session. Concerns which each brings to the group will, of course, be dealt with, but the leaders will emphasize existent reactions of those concerns, and will respond to the feelings of each member concerning the situation rather than responding to the situation itself.

Dialogue in the here and now:

Diane: "I'm really upset about what Joe did. He's mean and won't listen at all. He's impossible!"

Leader: "I'm receiving a lot of anger and frustration from you right now. I guess your statement about you is that you're pretty angry with Joe."

Each existent moment in group represents an Existential moment when a member (and a leader) will decide to define his essence with courage or will decide passively to resign his humanity. The courage to be requires that he live in continuous confrontation in and out of group with his being-in-the-world. His commitment to a decision-quality of human existence can be verbalized in the group. Living that commitment involves action outside the group.

Commitment stands on the statement, "This I am; this I believe; this I do. I am the being, the believing, the doing." Commitment is not a subscription to something external to one's life, but an awareness, an attitude, and a recognition of the feeling of being fully present in a moment, making choices in that moment, and standing on the consequences of those choices. Participation in life and in the group is a consequence of genuine committedness to living where one freely chooses one's being in action. If a person takes responsibility for his life and expresses it through participation, he is totally involved, totally committed (Bugenthal, 1965). A participant can practice participative behavior in the group life and perhaps increase involvement and commitment in life outside the group. The Extensional group is an arena where commitments can be articulated and extended into a member's entire life-space.

EXISTENTIAL CONCEPT: THE ENCOUNTER—THE "I-THOU" RELATIONSHIP DEFINES GROUP PROCESS AND CONTENT

When I think of the "I-Thou" relationship I become uneasy at times. What I must do to create this relationship is to communicate somehow my essence— open, uncensored, and vulnerable. I do not always want to do this, partly because it will be, as it must be, only a shadow of my "I-ness" and also because in reaching I-to-thou I am risking the pain of being misunderstood or unaccepted. I would rather be safe in my obscurity. I would like to hide behind an anonymous mask, then no other could encounter the "I" of me; nor I, the "Thou" of him. Thus we never meet—and hurt. But also, we never meet— and love.

Journey into Life Space. So I seek out the encounter "I-to-Thou," for here is where I exercise my being. In the encounter we live each other, reciprocating uniqueness and singularity. I enter the arena of another's life space, vulnerable to all that is there. I am not neutral, but am involved and committed. I risk pain and error, but I do this in awareness that encounter confirms my humanness, my authenticity, and my essence just as it confirms the humanity, authenticity, and essence of Thou—all mankind. As I comprehend the essence of another I take him into myself and allow myself to be taken into him, throwing open the gates of my being. We both experience an increasing inner richness.

This journey into the life space of Thou is not easy for me. I must lower my defenses, allow my shields to go down, and, in a curious fashion, turn myself off, partially losing awareness of myself as a being with needs, drives, and perceptions as I try to enter the awareness of another. I do not know exactly how I do this, except that the act, I know, requires deep concentration, intense involvement, and maximum energy on my part.

In and out of encounter I strive for perfect authenticity, but never am I complete, so I never outwardly transmit exactly what I am inwardly. I am never wholly congruent, but struggle constantly toward becoming, always in the process of self-actualizing, never self-actualized. This imperfection becomes a source of *angst,* of anxiety, to me. I would like to be completed, but I cannot attain total authenticity, which, I know, is as unattainable as total encounter.

26

IMPLICATIONS FOR THE EXTENSIONAL GROUP OF THE EXISTENTIAL CONCEPT: THE ENCOUNTER

In the I-Thou relationship, the group leader enters a member's life-space and shares that which he sees there. In openness and mutuality the Existentialist leader allows the worlds of the participants to unfold during an encounter. This requires that the leaders actively attempt to enter the members' worlds—not simply listen to them passively. The climate of the group is generated from empathy, congruency, and specificity on the part of the leader. Members are helped to experience existence as real, to increase their abilities to extend potentialities and expand alternatives. Each group member is assisted through the group process to sign his signature to his own statement of essence.

The Extensional leader views members of the group as unique, dynamic individuals, not as statistical norms. Each member is not an object to whom things are done, but a subject with whom action possibilities are explored. Each participant is treated with dignity as a *person,* whether he is child, adolescent, or adult. The leader encounters him, regardless of age, as a being of ultimate value—a person who, like the leader, is engaged in defining essence out of ambiguous freedom.

Journey into Life Space. Lewin's (1948) conceptualization of each individual existing in a life-space with parameters defined by the boundary which exists between self and the environment has application to the group process and relevancy to the Existential concept of Encounter. A person's life-space is dynamically a relatively closed system which attempts to maintain equilibrium under the impact of field forces, negative and positive valences. The various life-spheres (profession, family, friendships with definite persons, etc.) as well as different needs become more and more differentiated as a person expands his life-space and extends psychical regions and systems within his life-space.

Encounter involves explorations of an individual's life-space. As one group member describes the territory of his psychical sphere, other members and leaders "track" his verbalizations and in the process help that member understand, appreciate, and identify the forces in his idiosyncratic field. In a somewhat mystical sense, the experience of a group focusing on the life-space of one member illuminates that space with the group's energies. As group members journey into the

27

life-spaces of others in the group, human nourishment is given and received; but also insight concerning the realities of each individual's life space occurs. Somehow as group members and leaders "walk around" in one another's existences, obscured blocks to growth are identified and may then be dealt with. Characteristic life-styles can be identified also. A dialogue of such a journey is illustrated.

> *Harriet*: "I look around my world and it's all colored blue, and the people in it have dim faces. They aren't sad, but they aren't happy either."
>
> *Jerry*: "The way you describe it, they don't have much form, just seem to be blurs."
>
> *Harriet*: "Yeah, people really don't have much meaning for me. Sometimes I think I just use them to get out of them what I want but don't see a real person behind the face."
>
> *Leader*: "Like right now, for instance, you seem somehow cut off, kind of in the distance, not quite right here, and I'm wishing I could reach you."

Besides providing illumination to the life-space of each individual group member, the group process can be used to explore the relationship of one member's life-space to another's. It is essential that the group leader function actively during this experience. A leader's responsibility is to aid members to encounter one another, and to do this he must keep channels of communication open. He must insist that members make clear the hypotheses they might attempt to hide through using an interrogation form of speech. He refuses to allow one member to "hook" another on a question, but insists that the questioner make a statement about where he stands. The leader constantly emphasizes that each member is speaking only for himself. The leader encourages frequent use of "I's" on the part of group members. He insists that members talk face-to-face, never about another. He calls attention to members' reliance on the "they" world for legitimizing their personal stances and insists that each make his individual position clear. The leader translates generalities into concrete specifics. Part Two of this book addresses the functions of group leaders in detail.

SUMMARY STATEMENT: THE EXTENSIONAL GROUP

The preceding pages have identified some concepts of Existentialism which are relevant to the Extensional group. The philosophy has been presented from a personal point of view, then translated into implications for the Extensional group process. Illustrative dialogues have been provided.

FIGURE 1-2
PHILOSOPHICAL FRAMEWORK OF AN EXTENSIONAL GROUP

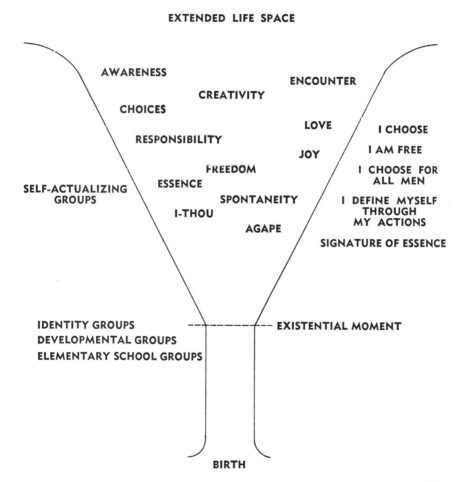

EXTENDED LIFE SPACE

AWARENESS

ENCOUNTER

CREATIVITY

CHOICES

LOVE

I CHOOSE

RESPONSIBILITY

JOY

I AM FREE

FREEDOM

I CHOOSE FOR ALL MEN

ESSENCE

SELF-ACTUALIZING GROUPS

SPONTANEITY

I DEFINE MYSELF THROUGH MY ACTIONS

I-THOU

AGAPE

SIGNATURE OF ESSENCE

IDENTITY GROUPS
DEVELOPMENTAL GROUPS
ELEMENTARY SCHOOL GROUPS — — — — — — EXISTENTIAL MOMENT

BIRTH

29

Group Leadership

The Extensional Group model is the theoretical paradigm on which this book is based. Figure 1-2 serves to summarize the philosophical framework of the Extensional Group. The theoretical foundations of other systems—psychoanalytical, phenomenological, behavioral—and a recapitulation of the Existentialist point of view have been provided in Appendix A, *Historical Foundations.* The cognitive map of the nature of man of each model, the group model, the leader's role, derived techniques, functions of group members, group members' goals and selected extensions of each model are provided. For the reader's convenience, an outline summarizing the material is also provided.

BIBLIOGRAPHY

Arbuckle, Dugald S. "Existentialism in Counseling: The Humanist View." *Personnel and Guidance Journal,* Vol. XLII, No. 6 (1965) , pp. 558-67.

Bach, George. "Marathon Group Dynamics: Dimensions of Helpfulness." *Psychological Reports,* Vol. XX, Southern Universities Press, 1967.

Bates, Marilyn, and Johnson, C. D. "The Existentialist Counselor at Work," *School Counselor,* March, 1969, pp. 245-250.

Beck, Carlton. *Philosophical Foundations of Guidance.* Englewood Cliffs, New Jersey: Prentice-Hall, 1963.

Berne, Eric. *Transactional Analysis.* New York: Grove Press, 1961.

Buber, Martin. *I and Thou.* New York: Charles Scribner's Sons, 1958.

Bugenthal, J. F. T. *The Search for Authenticity.* New York: Holt, Rinehart, and Winston, 1965.

Button, Alan DeWitt. *The Authentic Child.* New York: Random House, 1969.

Carkhuff, Robert R., and Berenson, Bernard C. *Beyond Counseling and Therapy.* New York: Holt, Rinehart & Winston, 1968.

Colm, Hanna. *The Existentialist Approach to Psychotherapy with Adults and Children.* New York: Grune & Stratton, 1966.

Dreyfus, Edward A. "Counseling and Existentialism," *Journal of Counseling Psychology.* Vol. IX, No. 2, pp. 128-34, 1962.

Eddy, William B., and Lubin, Bernard. "Laboratory Training and

Encounter Groups." *Personnel & Guidance Journal*, Vol. 49, #8, April 1971, pp. 625-634.

Erikson, Erik H. *Identity, Youth and Crisis.* New York: W. W. Norton, 1968.

Frankl, Viktor E. *The Doctor and the Soul.* New York: Alfred A. Knopf, 1965.

Frankl, Viktor E. *Man's Search for Meaning.* New York: Washington Press, 1963.

Goldberg, Carl. *Encounter: Group Sensitivity Training Experience.* New York: Science House, 1970.

Greenwald, Jerry A. "The Art of Emotional Nourishment: Self-Induced Nourishment and Toxicity." Unpublished Manuscript, Beverly Hills, Ca. n.d.

Harris, Thomas. *I'm Okay, You're Okay.* New York: McGraw-Hill, 1970.

Howard, Jane. *Please Touch.* New York: McGraw-Hill, 1970.

Johnson, Ernest L. "Existentialism, Self-Theory and the Existential Self." *Personnel and Guidance Journal,* Sept. 1967, pp. 53-58.

Kaufman, Walter, ed. *Existentialism from Dostoevsky to Sartre.* New York: Meridian Books, 1956.

Kierkegaard, Soren. *The Concept of Dread.* Translated by Walter Lowrie. Princeton, New Jersey: Princeton Univ. Press, 1944.

Kovacs, Arthur L. "The Intimate Relationship: A Therapeutic Paradox." *Journal of Psychotherapy.* Oct. 1965, pp. 97-103.

Lewin, Kurt. *A Dynamic Theory of Personality.* New York: McGraw-Hill, 1935.

Marcel, Gabriel. *The Philosophy of Existence.* London: Harvill, 1948.

Maslow, Abraham H. *Toward A Psychology of Being.* New York: Van Nostrand-Reinhold, 1968.

May, Rollo, ed. *Existential Psychology.* New York: Random House, 1961.

Morris, Van Cleve. *Existentialism in Education.* New York: Harper & Row, 1966.

Moustakas, Clark, ed. *Existential Child Therapy.* New York: Basic Books, 1966.

Redl, Fritz. *When We Deal With Children.* New York: The Free Press, 1966.

Sartre, Jean-Paul. *Existentialism and Human Emotions.* New York: Philosophical Library, 1957.

Shostrom, Everett L. "Group Therapy: Let the Buyer Beware." *Readings in Psychology Today.* Del Mar, Ca.: CRM Books, 1970, pp. 149-151.

Strickland, Ben. "Kierkegaard and Counseling for Individuality." *Personnel and Guidance Journal,* Jan. 1966, pp. 470-74.

Tillich, Paul. *The Courage to Be.* New Haven, Conn.: Yale Univ. Press, 1952.

Weisman, Avery D. *The Existential Core of Psychoanalysis.* Boston: Little, Brown, 1965.

Yalom, Irvin, and Lieberman, M. "Sensitivity Training: Caveat Emptor." *Behavior Today.* Vol. 2, #21, May 24, 1971.

CHAPTER 2

PARAMETERS OF THE GROUP PROCESSES

- Parameters of Student vs. Nonstudent Groups
- Parameters of Individuation and Enculturation Groups

To the Group Leader:

This chapter is designed to sort out the differences in your role as you lead various types of groups. Materials have been provided in Appendixes B, C, and D to help you function in these groups.

CHAPTER 2

PARAMETERS OF THE GROUP PROCESSES

Groups have been traditionally conceptualized as existing on a continuum with the process differentiated by the skills necessary to conduct groups at various levels of interaction. Teaching began at the cognitive end of the continuum while psychotherapy was placed as a polarity on the affective dimension. In this paradigm there lay the implication that the group process involved primarily depths of interaction varying in degrees of personal involvement by members and in degrees of training required of the group leader. The dynamics of the group process were conceptualized in this continuum model as being very similar and, basically, one process (See Figure 2-1).

The position of this overview is that the continuum paradigm is inaccurate and misleading. Rather, groups are seen as defined by a number of parameters whose boundaries vary from group to group. A more helpful way of looking at group processes might be to conceptualize them as spokes of a wheel radiating from a common core of learning (See Figure 2-2). All groups are seen as having been formed for the purpose of effecting a change of behavior (cognitive or affective) in the participants. This learning process may involve intellectual, perceptual, and conative changes. In some types of groups the parameters focus on enculturation; in other types of groups, focus is on individuation.

PARAMETERS OF STUDENT VS. NONSTUDENT GROUPS

The wheel diagram (Figure 2-2) suggests that the group processes radiate from and contribute to a learning core. These group processes can be diagrammed as directed to students or to nonstudents. *Student* and *nonstudent* in this sense relate to the educational or noneducational location of the group. Some group processes are appriate for students in public schools and institutional settings, while

FIGURE 2-1
TRADITIONAL CONCEPTUALIZATION OF THE GROUP PROCESS
A MISLEADING CONTINUUM

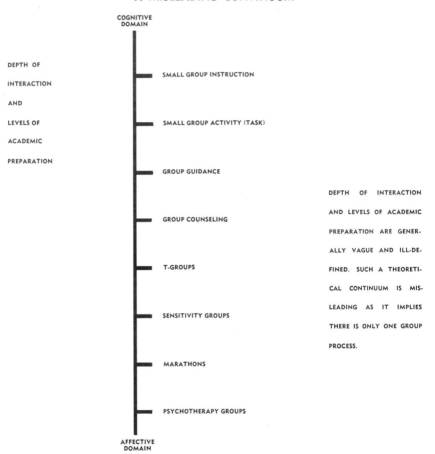

other group processes are appropriate for "nonstudents" only. Group counseling, group guidance, task-oriented, and small instructional groups are specific to public institutions. These groups should be conducted within different parameters from groups outside public schools, not only because schools are public institutions dealing with minors, but also, because students of public school age generally do not possess the ego strength necessary to handle the level of interaction characteristic of the encounter-type group. After the identity crisis of the later teens is negotiated, however, the sense of self solidi-

FIGURE 2-2

MODERN PARADIGM OF GROUP PROCESSES

DIRECTED TOWARD STUDENTS | **DIRECTED TOWARD NONSTUDENTS**

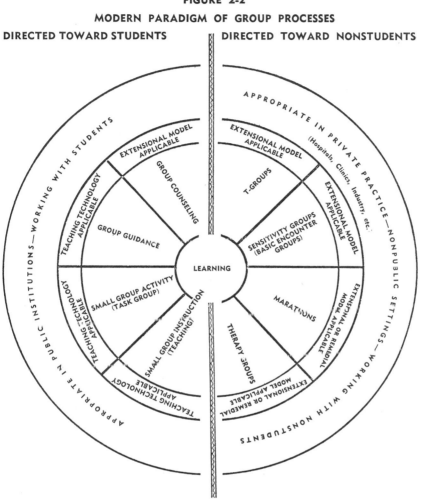

fies and strengthens, and psychological resources probably are sufficient to benefit from exploration of the sensitivity-type group. Until
this occurs, the group leader must modify his behavior to create
group processes which are appropriate for the young person still in a
developmental stage and not psychologically mature.

Encounter groups, T-groups, sensitivity groups, and therapy groups
are relevant to hospitals, clinics, industry, and private practices where
the purpose is to enable participants to become more self-actualizing,
or to improve coping mechanisms.

Group Leadership

All the processes contribute to learning and all to some degree involve different skills on the part of the group leader. Depending on the purposes of the group, the setting in which it is conducted, and the composition of group membership, group leaders should activate different dynamics. For example, in a group-guidance group the leader should have in mind information he wishes to transmit to the group as a whole, and therefore while he uses dynamics of group interaction, he also has a group goal (enculturation) which is primarily in the cognitive domain. On the other hand, in a counseling group, the leader should emphasize individual goals and focus on individual growth (individuation). He uses group dynamics which very likely emphasize the affective (conative) domain more than the cognitive domain.

If group-guidance or group-counseling groups are conducted in a public school setting with minors, the group leader should be sensitive to content which may violate the privacy of the family. The leader should be very aware that this type of group *cannot* assume the degree of confidentiality which groups held outside the public school setting and involving nonstudents can assume. Therefore, content which may be explored in a sensitivity or therapy group may not be appropriate for a public school student group. The parameters which define the boundaries within which a group operates are governed to some extent by the setting; thus, the group leader must be able to activate those dynamics which are suitable for the type of group he is leading.

PARAMETERS OF INDIVIDUATION AND ENCULTURATION GROUPS

The Extensional model, where focus is on individuation, and the Remedial model, where the initial focus is on remedial enculturation, have been contrasted in the first chapter of this manual and are applicable to groups in and out of institutional settings. The Extensional model is appropriate for Group Counseling, T-groups, and Encounter groups, while either the Extensional or Remedial model may be appropriate for marathons or therapy groups. The leader makes this professional decision based on the needs of his group members.

To achieve enculturating goals in group guidance, small group activities and small group instruction, modern teaching technology is applicable. The leader of these three types of group processes will select the approaches which best suit the group goals. Discussion techniques, decision-making analyses, simulations, games, multi-media stimuli such as slides, tape recordings, films and film strips, role-playing, self-assessment procedures, vocational exploration, and problem-centered groups composed of students labeled by the school as "attendance problems," "underachievers," "disruptive behavior problems," "failures," etc. may be the focus of these groups. All three of these types of groups are aimed at *enculturating* the student, that is, helping him to learn mores which enable him to cope with the demands of the culture, and to become a functioning, productive member of that culture. An effective enculturating process is essential for any society if it is to survive. The *primary* focus of all institutions, educational and otherwise, must and should be on enculturation.

Fortunately, there is recognition in our culture that the individuation process is equally important; that is, a recognition that each individual within a culture is unique, is in some way different from anyone else and that these differences can be a valuable resource to his culture. Culturation must be effected to some degree before *primary* focus can be on individuation, or a society would be in chaos. But if *only* culturation were achieved, a society would be changeless.

The *primary* focus of groups where the Extensional Model is appropriate is that of individuation. In these groups, the unique qualities of each participant are explored. Each member examines his values, his priorities, his individual strengths, and his individual life style. Content focuses on how members differ one from another and what each can do with his differences. Thus it is illogical to expect that a group measure can be used to determine effectiveness of the group process. Rather, assessment must be on an individual basis, with the instrumentation individually selected in the pre-group interview. Leaders of Extensional groups which focus on individuation *can* be accountable for midwifing the group process; they cannot be accountable for unilaterally specifying the goals of individuation. This must be done by the individual member with the help of the leader since these goals and objectives are idiosyncratic if consistent with the concept of individuation.

The reader will observe that "primary" in the two preceding paragraphs has been italicized. The intent is to emphasize that both enculturation and individuation processes interweave and are complementary. No precise line of demarcation can be drawn between the two processes, but the group which addresses as its *main* focus the enculturation of values, mores, and conventions of society is obviously different from the group which has as its main focus bringing into the awareness of each participant how *his* values and behaviors total to a unique life style, one which he is responsible for defining and translating into action.

Definitions of Group Processes. A description of the various types of groups appropriate to public schools, or institutions dealing with minors, and the types of groups appropriate outside public schools, is located in Appendix B. A definition of each type of group and its goals are presented, and the dynamics which the leader should activate in the various types of groups are specified. A suggested minimal level of training necessary to lead such groups in a professional manner is summarized, followed by a description of specialized materials available for the leader's use. Appendix C contains a listing of literature which serves as a resource bibliography for the various categories of groups. These have been arranged to reflect the divisions made in Figure 2-2—"Modern Paradigm of Group Processes." Appendix D provides an annotation of specialized materials for the various types of groups, following the same categories as Appendices B and C.

CHAPTER 3

THE ROLES OF THE LEADERS

- The Nature of the Leaders
    Maintenance Groups
    Co-Counselor Model
- The Nature of the Leader's Techniques
    Confrontation—an Act of Grace
    Attending Behavior
    Feedback
    Misuse of Questions as a Technique
    Levels of Interaction
    Opening a Session
    Closing a Session
    Capping
- Summary
- Bibliography

To the Group Leader:

You, as group leader, are the keystone of interaction. Who you are is primary. What you do is who you are. You are your technique.

CHAPTER 3

THE ROLES OF THE LEADERS

THE NATURE OF THE LEADERS

A counseling group draws definition from its leader. It will be only as good as the leader, as good as his skills, and as good as the being of the leader himself. A person may be competent in the technical aspects of group leadership, but if he himself is not a "good" human being, his groups can become destructive. Whether a leader is working with a Remedial group or an Extensional group, it is important that he is a nourishing human being. If he is a toxic human being, he may, as Greenwald (n.d.) suggests, "suck" nourishment out of others. A group led by a toxic leader may be unhealthy for participants while a group led by a nourishing leader can be enriching. If, as Greenwald claims, toxic people radiate their deadliness to others who are exposed to them, a depressed, hostile leader may radiate his depression throughout a group. A nourishing leader, on the other hand, thrives on joyous human interaction and is a self-nourisher who will generate his own enrichment rather than feeding off group members.

Maintenance Groups

An implication of Greenwald's (ibid.) constructs of toxic and nourishing people is the importance of a maintenance group for the group leader in which he participates as a group member. If, as Greenwald claims, toxicity is contagious, and since inevitably groups will contain some toxic members, it is imperative that group leaders plan a program for the maintenance of their own psychological well-being. It is suggested by the writers of this manual that a group be formed for the purpose of maintaining growth toward self-actualization. Such a Maintenance Group would consist of professional group leaders who meet twice monthly and rotate leadership each time. The agenda would be the inward exploration of self to maintain and consolidate growth gains.

The Co-counselor Model

It is also the conviction of the writers that the co-counselor model provides the most effective model of group leadership. This format offers a way to attain productivity in a group with maximum control of the process and a minimum of risk and control of members.

The male-female co-counselor model is preferred, but a dyadic model of the same sex may be as satisfactory. Regardless of sex the team must be complementary and must work from the same theoretical orientation. Teams who first work together may experience some difficulty in trusting each other and in understanding the other's mode of functioning, but within two sessions those who will find the relationship comfortable have learned to work with each other.

Co-counselors who have had successful experience in this model find it more satisfactory than single leadership. One satisfaction stems from the post-group critique which co-counselors hold. Areas of concern, areas of success, and areas which need to be explored can be discussed by the team immediately after a session. Instant feedback can be given concerning the leadership of the group session.

Another satisfaction with the model lies in the "anchor" one member of the team provides while the other member is engaged in intensive interaction with one or several members of the group. When one of the group leaders focuses very deeply into the life space of an individual member, inevitably this leader loses monitoring of the group. In the co-counselor model the other leader can maintain this function, thus insuring the ongoing safety of the group.

A third advantage of the co-counselor model is that it provides a model of confrontation without risking a group member. Co-leaders are expendable to each other and the group, and can use one another to model confrontation early in group life at a depth which might be unwise if the interaction were taking place between leader and member.

A fourth asset of the co-counselor model is the constant check each has for the counter-transferences, self-needs, distortions stemming from biases, inaccuracies, and inadequacies of the other. Each co-counselor can keep the other "honest" and give feedback concerning inauthentic behavior.

The co-counselors should position themselves across from one another in the group circle and either can begin the session. The productivity level of the group can be maintained by the constant interaction of two leaders. Groups led by co-counselors tend to move rapidly and to sustain intense interaction throughout a session. According to a study reported in *Frontiers of Hospital Psychiatry* (1970) concerning the use of co-therapists in large group therapy, co-leaders kept the sessions from becoming intellectual or dull, and as the therapists became more comfortable working together they were able to lead one another away from unproductive areas and to sense group affect which might have been missed had they been operating alone. This study found that some leaders emerged as more capable of handling anger, depressions, or resistances while others showed greater skill at being supportive. A major advantage of the use of more than one group leader was the enhanced ability to penetrate members' resistances and quickly to reach significant affect-laden material. Working together, the co-leaders did not allow members to dwell on areas they knew were unproductive, i.e., conventional-general topic on *HIM* (Hill, 1965), but could move them to meaningful material rapidly. The use of co-leaders in large group therapy also was seen as an opportunity to train beginning group leaders by providing them with a setting in which they could work across from an experienced leader.

Two dialogues illustrating co-leaders' interaction are provided, one involving students, one involving adults:

Member:
(Mike)
"John, you just burn me up because of your being dishonest all the time."

Co-leader:
#1
"Mike, you seem angry with John. Tell John exactly what you think about him."

Co-leader:
#2
(To Co-leader #1) "I don't like what you are doing. You are manipulating Mike against John and it seems to me it would be more helpful to the group if you dealt with your feelings."

45

Member: (Lois)	(To Co-Counselor #1) "You refuse to deal with my anger and hostilities. You constantly duck the issue and refuse to deal with me."
Co-leader: #2	"Lois, you're so overwhelmed with your feelings that you can't seem to clarify them and I would like to deal with you and have you tell me what's going on."
Lois:	"I can't seem to get any response or emotion from Co-leader #1."
Co-leader: #1	"It seems to me, Lois, that you somehow want me to pick up and swallow your anger and hostility. I react that if I did that, we would both be angry, and I can't see what help that is to either of us."

THE NATURE OF THE LEADER'S TECHNIQUES

It is quite true that a leader can possess brilliant techniques but still be ineffective. Techniques are tools which are only as good as the user. The nature of the leader is primary; this is his art. The nature of a leader's techniques is secondary; this is his science. It is the thrust of this section to delineate some of the verbal dimensions of group interaction which constitute that science: confrontation, attending behavior, feedback, use of questions, levels of interaction, and opening and closing a session. The four functions of group leaders will be analyzed in detail in a succeeding chapter.

Confrontation—An Act of Grace

Confrontation offered with empathy is an act of grace. Confrontation offered with animosity is a graceless act. The line which divides the two lies within the confronter. His caring, unconditional, positive regard, his congruency, his authenticity, his *agape* (tax-free love) render confrontation a gift of great value. Without these characteristics confrontation becomes twisted by hostility and diminishes both receiver and sender.

Both Hill (ibid.) and Bach (1967) have identified confrontation as a helpful dimension in verbal interaction. *The Hill Interaction Matrix* assigns the highest level of productivity in group interaction to the Confrontation—Personal Cell IV-D and Confrontation—Relationship Cell IV-E (Hill, ibid.). Anderson (1968) has provided additional understanding of the impact of confrontation. She has found that, *if* the counselor operates with a high degree of empathy, with positive regard for the client, genuineness, concreteness, and self-disclosure, the offering of confrontation will be facilitating; if, on the other hand, the counselor operates at low levels of empathy, does not truly care for the client, and is inauthentic and fearful of risking himself, confrontation will be experienced by the client as criticizing, unfeeling, and overly intellectual. Counselors who consistently operate at a high level of interaction tend to respond to the strengths and resources of a client, while counselors who tend to function at a low level respond to the counselee's weaknesses.

The bench mark of confrontation is the risk the leader takes with himself as he makes the verbal offering. In confrontation he will state clearly his position, his feelings, his perceptions, and will state them in the here and now; and these will be discrepant with those offered by the counselee. For example, a counselee might say, "I couldn't do my homework again last night, because the teacher didn't make it clear, and anyway, I forgot to take my book home. Besides, there was too much noise in the house, because my dad and mom were looking at TV." A confrontation might be, "I'm feeling pretty irritated by your comment. I think you are blaming everyone else and never intended to do the work." In this confrontation the counselee knows the counselor disagrees with him and feels somewhat angry at that moment, yet the counselee also knows that the counselor cared enough to risk himself in a way which could cause the counselee to reject him and turn on him in anger.

Confrontation differs from interpretation in that in the latter the counselor makes an observation based on some theoretical postulate. For example, if the counselor had wished to interpret the counselee's comment about his homework, he might have said, "I think you are rationalizing all around the issue. You are giving *good* reasons, but not the real ones." Interpretation often tends to focus on the past, i.e., search for explanations of behaviors in previous occurrences; while confrontation always focuses on the existent moment—dealing with how it is with counselor—counselee (s). On the *HIM* (Hill, ibid.) the speculative mode usually generates a great deal of interpretation.

47

Both confrontation and interpretation, however, consist of content to which a counselee can react emotionally and perhaps gain insight into his own functioning.

Anderson (1968: 411) stated that a confrontation can be said to have occurred if:

1. The client describes himself to the therapist in terms of what he wishes to be (his ego-ideal) rather than what he is (his real self), whereupon the therapist faces the client with his own experience of the situation.
2. The client expresses an increased awareness of himself (insight) as if this were the magical solution to all his problems; that is, there is a discrepancy between the client's insights and his actions in relation to these insights.

Confrontation is an act of grace, as in this process the confronter risks himself, but in so doing sends a message to the receiver that he, the confronter, cares enough to take that risk and respects the integrity and self-determination of the receiver. The confronter is saying, "I respect you, I value you, and I believe you have the strength to receive me fully—uncensored and giving all of myself, my reactions and my perceptions. Knowing that you may reject me, I am giving you some of my essence; I do this because I care for you."

Two dialogues serve to represent confrontation in group interaction.

Dick: "I don't like you, Mary. You are a manipulating female and you make me mad."

Mary: "Dick, I experience you as using me to get rid of your hostilities toward women and I don't like for you to do that."

Ken: "That dumb teacher picks on me all the time."

Edsel: "Aw, Ken, you bring it on yourself and you make me mad when you make statements like that. You cause the trouble and you try to blame the teacher."

Attending Behavior

The group leader may not be aware of some of his nonverbal messages, particularly those which transmit attending or nonattending behavior. The use of videotape recordings can be useful in increasing the leader's awareness of this kind of behavior. (See chapter 9 on "The Use of Videotape Confrontation.")

Ivey, et al. (1968), have used attending behavior as their initial focus in microcounseling—working with the one-to-one relationship —but, again, their observations are relevant to the work of the group leader. Three central aspects of attending behavior have been identified with both verbal and nonverbal components.

The first is eye contact. If the group leader does not maintain eye contact with his members, they are likely to feel they are being treated as objects rather than subjects. A major vehicle for transmitting empathy is eye contact; thus, it is important that the group leader be very aware of what he is doing with his eye language.

A second component of attending behavior concerns postural movement and gestures. The group leader can transmit "I hear, I understand, I feel" through his body posture.

The third element, verbal following behavior, also transmits attending or nonattending. The beginning counselor has difficulty "tracking" accurately the outputs of a counselee in a one-to-one relationship, and it is infinitely more difficult to track accurately the outputs of members of a group, yet this is what a group leader must do, and he must respond in a way that allows group members to know they are being heard. The leader should respond easily in a variety of modes: reflection of content, reflection of feeling, clarification, and general leads.

Feedback

The giving and receiving of feedback is the life stream of a group without which it has no reason for existing, yet the leader cannot assume that members are sensitive to this kind of communication. Generally in our daily lives we receive little feedback, and almost never the honest kind which is the *sine qua non* of group life; thus, people blindly persevere in the same mistakes day after day. Even though a person may be dimly aware that something is amiss in his behavior, seldom can he specify exactly which behaviors are causing his discomfort. He does not know concretely what he is doing that causes unwanted reactions in others. Consequently, he does not possess the raw materials of change—awareness of unwanted behaviors.

It is no accident that we do not routinely give and receive feedback in our daily lives. To do so is extremely difficult, and involves a personal risk which most people are not willing to take. It also involves a commitment to another human being, which is indeed rare; *and* it requires a skill not commonly possessed.

If group members are going to learn how to give and receive feedback, the group leader must transmit this information through modeling in his own behavior and, perhaps, through direct instruction. One tool has already been provided in this manual concerning teaching group members to give and receive feedback—"The Open Letter." The leader may, however, wish to reinforce the concepts contained in this letter early in the group life.

Feedback is not always helpful, and the leader needs to be alert to motives behind members' feedback offerings. Often the material is rejecting rather than confrontive and the primary motivation is to punish another group member in some way or to make the giver of the feedback feel better. If these situations occur, it is the leader's responsibility to call attention to his own reaction to the feedback and question the motivation. Members may practice "groupsmanship" in the guise of feedback, using their verbalizations to demonstrate how sophisticated, perceptive, or brilliant they are.

Then again, feedback may be motivated by a caring for another and a willingness to share oneself, and feedback may be created with courage to take a risk. Authentic feedback, as in confrontation, is an act of grace.

Feedback must be specific to be helpful and must deal with behaviors which are *current* and which can be changed. For example, if a member comments to another, "I think you are very unfriendly," the leader will ask the member to specify exactly what behaviors of this "unfriendly" member gave him such an impression. (And, as always, the leader emphasizes that in all our statements we are essentially talking about ourselves!)

Feedback is verbalized so that it is clearly from the frame of reference of the person offering the feedback. Thus, "I am getting tense

50

sitting next to you as you have been tapping your foot for several minutes," would be preferable to "You are tense tonight. What is the matter?" The leader may need to intervene frequently, early in a group's life, to insist that speakers do speak from their own point of view—where they are at—rather than place the focus of their comments on the member who is the target of the feedback. As members learn how to give self-centered feedback, however, the leader's intervention activities can subside.

Feedback must not be perceived as a mandate for change. Over and over the leader must emphasize that the giver of feedback is saying how it is with him and the receiver may do with the comments what he will. If he chooses to change, it must be because *he* wants to, not because other members of the group "suggest" that he do so. It ought to be clear to every member that no one has the right to ask another to change. *Feedback only transmits information of how it is with the sender; it does not solicit changes on the part of the receiver.*

A curious situation often occurs in the giving of pseudo-feedback. A member might comment to another, "I used to find you cold and unfeeling, but now I find you warmer," and then wait expectantly for a response from the person to whom the comment was directed. The receiving person inevitably feels a burden is placed on him and he is expected to do something with it. In actuality he is left with no place to go, except an inane "That's nice," or a rude "So?", or an uncomfortable, "I like you, too." The original comment was a subtle form of "Groupsmanship" which is difficult for the leader to handle without seeming to reprimand. He could call attention to the comment's hook of when-did-you-stop-beating-your-wife ploy or he could intervene with a comment on how the pseudo-feedback made *him* feel. The giver of the pseudo-feedback probably had good intentions, but this kind of interaction is *not* authentic feedback. The latter always has a handle on it which enables the receiver to deal with it and respond to it. Using the above example, real feedback might have gone like this: "I feel bad that I used to see you as cold and uncaring and would like to ask for your understanding of my blind spot." In this case the receiver is left with a handle by which to respond and the interaction can continue.

Group interaction is based on feedback. The effectiveness of a group depends on the quality of the feedback contained in the interaction, and it is the group leader's responsibility to control the quality of the feedback. From honest, helpful feedback a group member may gain self-understanding and increased awareness of the effects of certain of his behaviors on others; he may become more sensitive to contradictions between his verbal and nonverbal messages, may come to understand distortions in his communication patterns, may understand better his projections, and may experience heightened sense of self as a delightful, exciting, warm, and loving human being.

Three examples of feedback dialogue:

Leslie: "I wish someone would help me understand how I'm coming on 'child.' "

Clarence: "You ask questions when you really know the answer."

Don: "You sit in a little girl way. . . ."

Leader: "It would be helpful if you were more specific."
(To Don)

Don: "Well, Leslie, you fold your hands in your lap and you tip your head to one side when you are coming on child."

———

Member: "I don't like coming to you as a counselor because you never seem to have time for me. I put in a request and what you do I don't know because I don't get to see you. . . ."
(Bob)

Co-leader: "Bob, you are attacking me and I don't know what to say."
#1

Co-leader: "It seems to me, Co-leader # 1, I experience you as being on the spot and not knowing how to handle it. Some feedback about how you are feeling might be helpful."
#2

———

George: "I tried out for the football team but the coach has favorites and I don't ever get to play. . . ."

Sandy: "George, you hardly ever turn up for practice, you
                fool around during line-up, you don't follow team
                rules—I don't really think you can make it and this
                is your way of getting out of it. . . ."

Misuse of Questions as a Technique

The leader must be equipped to control the group process but *not*
the members of the group. The trap inherent in the use of questions as a leadership technique is that it *does* control the members.
The most efficient method of keeping members in submission is to
interrogate them. The leader need never allow his position to be
known but is always the "Authority" who graciously doles out bits
of wisdom at the appropriate time. The leader can exercise iron
control over members through firing questions at them, particularly
"Why?" questions (see "The Advanced Art of Groupsmanship").
Members will experience themselves as objects and the leader will be
relating to them as objects—things to be manipulated, not persons
to be known.

It will probably be more difficult for the leader to eliminate questions from his own verbal behavior than to eliminate questions on
the part of group members. In the former instance the leader may
be giving up his only method of control—his entire repertoire of
group leadership. In the latter instance all the leader need do is to
insist that a member rephrase a question into a statement, making
clear his position regarding the comment. For example a member
might query, "Why didn't you ask the teacher for permission to leave
the room?" The leader's responsibility is to intervene and insist that
the member asking the question make a statement concerning his position, or thought, or assumption behind the question. In response to
the leader's request that the thought behind the question be made
clear, the questioner might say, "I think you should have asked the
teacher for permission to leave the room." Again the "hook" of the
question has been turned into a "handle" to which a receiver can
respond. The leader should permit questions on his part or on the
part of group members *only* when the asker needs the information,
such as, "Are we meeting next Tuesday?" He also should be aware
that questions tend to probe into the Private Life Space, Cell III of
the Johari Window. Even such a simple question as "What did you

do last night?" may trespass and the leader must intervene by asking the questioner to volunteer where *he* is here and now, rather than volunteering another member's life space.

Levels of Interaction

Carkhuff and Berenson (1967) have identified five levels of responses with the one-to-one counseling relationship in mind, but these same levels seem to apply to the group leader's functioning. These levels range from one, the lowest level, to five, the most accurate level of interaction.

At Level 1 a response will either reflect that the group leader did not attend to the communication of a member, or the leader's response detracted significantly from the member's expression. For example, a member might say, "I just can't seem to get along with my wife." A Level 1 response might be for the leader to comment, "Where does she work?"

At Level 2 the leader's responses will subtract noticeably from the feelings communicated by a member. Thus, in response to a comment such as "I just can't get along with my wife," the leader might state, "How long have you two been married?"

At Level 3 the leader's response adds to the statement of a member, but essentially is interchangeable and does not help a group member understand what he is saying. In response to "I just can't get along with my wife," the leader might respond with, "The two of you just seem to be at odds." In this case the leader's remark had essentially the same affect and the same meaning, but did not subtract from the member's comment.

Level 4 responses finds the leader adding noticeably to the expressions of members in such a way as to express feelings a level deeper than those of the member. To "I just can't seem to get along with my wife," the leader might respond, "You are feeling pretty despondent about the whole situation and don't quite know what to do about it." The leader heard the feelings the member had not overtly verbalized and responded to them.

At Level 5 the leader's remarks add significantly to the feelings and meanings of the member in such a way as to express accurately levels of feeling below what the member himself is able to express. In responding to the example "I just can't seem to get along with my wife," the leader might reply, "I'm feeling almost a panic in you, a feeling of being closed in, pushed from all sides, trapped and going under deeper."

Carkhuff and Berenson's work (1967) is especially important in that they point out that the counselor who is not functioning at a more facilitative level than a counselee will harm the counselee. It seems logical that, if this is the case in the one-to-one relationship, it also is true for the group leader's relationship with his members. It also may be true for the interrelationships among members, and if this *is* the case, the necessity for the group leader to be able to control the group process cannot be overemphasized.

Opening a Session

The leader needs to have some general leads at his command which may be useful in opening the sessions. These might be: "We can begin anywhere you like," "Let's get started," or "It's time to begin." These statements simply give the signal that the group is in session.

The leader also may want to use some of the confrontation tech niques (verbal and nonverbal) to begin a group, but there is danger that a group will tend to become dependent on the leader always to initiate interaction. If the leader allows this to happen, he is taking away from the members the opportunity to develop independence and autonomy; therefore, if the leader chooses to use some interaction stimulators one time, he should be wary of taking complete responsibility for initiating interaction the next.

The leader also may begin a group with silence, waiting for a member to initiate verbal communication. The danger here is that the silence can become punitive and, if this occurs, the leader has the responsibility of breaking the silence. He might do this by sharing where *he* is, and how *he* feels. The leader has no more right to volunteer a member than one member has the right to volunteer another. The only legitimate tool the leader has to model "here and now" behaviors is himself or the co-leader. This is not to imply that the leader ever becomes a member of a group—he is *always* the leader; he is there for the gain of the members. The leader must join his own growth or maintenance group when he wishes to become a member.

The "go-around" is helpful to open a session. The leader suggests the go-around which might be for each to share how he is feeling at that very minute. After he makes the original suggestion, he continues to comment for a few seconds, having made clear where the go-around will begin and the direction it will go. He can initiate the experience by sharing himself, ask for feedback, then encourage the others to participate. The reason for the delay between the suggestion and implementation is to give members a moment to prepare themselves; to marshal their thoughts—in other words, to avoid surprises which generate defensive reactions.

The beginning group leader often makes the mistake of assuming that a group begins one session where it left off the last. This is in error. When a group parts, each member (and leader) will continue the internal dialogue with self for many, many hours. During these "conversations" growth takes place; insights occur, understandings develop. Thus, it is naive for the group leader to assume that a group will begin where it ended; rather, the leader should make the assumption that the group members are in quite a different place from where they left off. He attempts to begin each session, then, in the here and now, making no assumptions about the there and then.

Closing a Session

Groups must begin and end on time. The logic of this is that through groups members test and learn limits, and if the leader removes the agreed-upon limits, he is abdicating his responsibility, reinforcing a perception many of the group members may already have —that people often don't mean what they say, i.e., cannot be trusted. The same rationale applies to the number of sessions. An eight-session group is just that— not an eight-plus-two-plus-? group. The neophyte group leader will have difficulty with both beginning and ending an individual group session on time and terminating the group itself, but, as he gains experience, he will realize the importance of doing both.

Capping

Since the leader ends at a previously agreed time, he needs a technique to bring the group back to the nongroup world—the real, outside world. He does this through *capping*. Somewhere near the end of a session the leader begins easing up interaction from the lower cells of the *HIM* to the conventional cells. Emotional content is tapered off and cognitive processes made dominant. The leader does this by responding deliberately to *ideas* and *generalities*, responding to cognitive content rather than conative content. Thus, the group is brought away from deep emotional exploration and is prepared to function in their usual life-spaces in the world of social reality. The amount of time the leader needs for this process depends on the sophistication of the group, the destination of members when they leave the group (e.g., home, classroom, job, or lunch), and the depths of interaction at which the group was working. There may be times when the leader does not wish to cap, but he has to make sure that no member is left in a state of crisis. No member should leave a group session unable to cope with his world; it is the group leader's responsibility to see that this does *not* happen. At the same time he does not want to close the door on a member's growth, which (unfortunately) usually involves some discomfort. The leader's art of group leadership must be brought into play to help him know when a member is being left in a state of crisis or with an unresolved concern on which he needs to work. A leader with an obsessive need for closure may have difficulty with this decision.

At the end of every session the leader may wish to "go around" and give each member an opportunity to make a final comment. A member may want to direct a remark to a particular member or to the group as a whole, or he may not wish to speak. At this point the leader does not stimulate interaction but only responds as absolutely necessary.

A leader may wish to have members write logs at the end of every session. A 5" x 8" card titled "Group Reflections" presents a useful format. The cards are signed so that the leader can keep in touch with each member. These logs are never read aloud to the group or referred to in the group by the leader.

SUMMARY

This chapter has presented comments regarding the nature of the group leader, emphasizing the importance of the leader's own personal level of interaction with implications for the ability to provide human nourishment. The co-counselor paradigm was advanced as the most effective model in achieving maximum group productivity in a minimum amount of time.

The nature of the group leader's techniques was discussed as they concerned the level of interaction, the use of confrontation, the components of attending behaviors, the use and misuse of feedback as the *sine qua non* of group life, and the misuse of questions as a technique. Procedures for opening and closing sessions with an additional section on capping completed the chapter.

BIBLIOGRAPHY

Anderson, Susan C. "Effects of Confrontation by High-and-Low-Functioning Therapists," *Journal of Counseling Psychology,* Vol. 15, #5, 1968, pp. 411-416.

Bach, George. "Marathon Group Dynamics: Dimensions of Helpfulness." *Psychological Reports* 20, Southern Universities Press, 1967, pp. 1147-1158.

Carkhuff, Robert R., and Berenson, Bernard G. *Beyond Counseling and Therapy.* New York: Holt, Rinehart and Winston, 1967.

Greenwald, Jerry A. "The Art of Emotional Nourishment: Self-Induced Nourishment and Toxicity." Unpublished Manuscript. Jerry Greenwald, Ph.D., 450 N. Bedford Drive, Beverly Hills, California. n.d.

Herscheiman, Philip, and Freundich, David. "Large Group Therapy Seen as an Improvement over Ward Meetings." *Frontiers of Hospital Psychiatry,* Vol. 7, No. 11. Published by the Roche Laboratories, Division of Hoffman-La Roche, Inc., Nutley, New Jersey. World Wide Medical Press, June 1, 1970.

Hill, William Fawcett. *Hill Interaction Maxtrix.* Los Angeles Youth Studies Center, University of Southern California, 1965.

Ivey, Allen E.; Normington, Cheryl J.; Miller, C. Dean; Morrill, Weston, H.; and Haase, Richard R. "Micro-counseling and Attending Behavior: An Approach to Prepracticum Counselor Training." *Journal of Counseling Psychology,* Vol. 15, No. 5, Part 2, Sept., 1968. Monograph Supplement.

Lee, Nancy V. *Verbal Dimensions of Counseling.* Unpublished Master's Thesis, California State College, Fullerton, 1968.

CHAPTER 4

A MICROANALYSIS OF THE FUNCTIONS OF GROUP LEADERSHIP

- Traffic Directing
    Blocking Questions
    Blocking "Gossip"
    Blocking the There and Then
    Blocking "Super-Mothering"
    Blocking Mind-raping
    Blocking Invasion of Privacy
- Modeling
- Interaction Catalyst
- Communication Facilitator
    Reflecting Content
    Linking
    Reflecting Feelings
    The Ears of the Leaders
    Communication Patterns to Avoid
- Summary

To the Group Leader:

This microanalysis takes the functions of group leadership apart. You must reassemble into your own unique gestalt.

CHAPTER 4

A MICROANALYSIS OF THE FUNCTIONS OF GROUP LEADERSHIP

The role of the extensional co-leader is characterized by professional expertise coupled with clear acceptance of the responsibility of leadership. The person of the co-leader, in the final analysis, defines the role. Who he is, his authenticity, his awareness, his degree of self-actualization, his empathy, his intelligence, his self-acceptance, in short his "human-ness," is the most relevant variable that he brings to group leadership. Without these sensitivities, professional expertise is gratuitous. Without professional expertise, the sensitivities are also gratuitous. A knowledge of the functions of group leadership is essential preparation for the role of co-leaders.

These functions are analyzed in detail in this chapter. A micro-approach has been taken to isolate their components, but it cannot be overemphasized that the functions interrelate, complementing and supplementing one another. The whole of co-leadership is a great deal more than the sum of the components. Each co-leader must go through his own process of synthesizing and integrating these functions into a gestalt. The intent of this chapter is to specify the four micro-elements which seem to the writers to compose the gestalt of co-leadership. These elements are: functions of traffic directing; modeling; interaction catalyst; and communication facilitator.

TRAFFIC-DIRECTING

One of the functions which requires a fair amount of attention early in a group's life is that of traffic-directing. The co-leaders will need to help members become aware of behaviors which open communication channels and those which inhibit communication, and this function will need active attention as the group begins its initial interaction efforts. As members learn group membership responsibility, traffic-directing interventions of the co-leaders will diminish. Those few which will be required after the first sessions probably will be performed by the members themselves.

Blocking Questions

A vital traffic-directing function which will meet with the most resistance is that of blocking questions. Out-group speech patterns rely heavily on the questioning form of communication. The awareness that questioners control the responder in a very subtle way is only dimly perceived by most people. The majority of group members will bring to the group a heavy reliance on questions as a way of communicating. Co-leaders take away this self-protective, defensive "crutch" when they ask a member to abandon his traditional way of controlling others through the "hooks" of questions, and come out in the open with a clear statement of where he is. At first, the member inevitably feels angry and hostile and will evidence impatience and resistance. Co-leaders will have to determine when the price of intervention in terms of irritation to members will be inhibiting or facilitating, and use their judgments as to when to intervene and when to abstain. The blocking of questions must be done gently, without rejecting the questioner.

An example might be:

John: (member)	"Why do you feel like that, Paul?"
Co-leader: (Intervention)	"John, you have phrased your concern so that Paul doesn't know how it is with you. I feel it will be more helpful if you make it clear what you have in mind."
John:	"Paul, I guess I don't relate to what you are saying because I don't think I would feel that way."
	(John's first statement implies judgment. His second statement is a clear message of where he stands concerning the issue and with Paul.)

Mary: "How do you feel about it, Ralph?"
(Member)

Co-leader: "I wish you would make it clear to Ralph how
(Intervention)   you feel about it, Mary."

Mary: "You make me mad, Ralph, I want you to say
how you feel about the situation and I'm irritated
with you because you haven't."

Blocking Gossip

Blocking "gossip" is far easier than blocking questions. In the
latter the co-leader will be working against an ingrained speech
pattern which involves a valued control of others. In the former,
members are talking *about* another member rather than directly *to
him*. For example, one member will be referring to something which
occurred, or a reaction, or a concern which involves another member,
and will address still another member or the group as a whole. The
co-leader needs to intervene and direct the member to speak directly
to the other member concerned.

There is an inherent inconsistency in the co-leader's intervention
in blocking "gossiping." When he directs one member to speak
directly to another member, rather than speaking about him, the co-
leader is speaking *about* the other member. This problem seems
imbedded in the English language and appears to be a necessary case
of "Don't do as I do, but as I say," on the part of the co-leader as he
intervenes. One way to handle this inconsistency is to call the group's
attention to the necessity for the leader's intervention being stated in
the third person while he is asking members to communicate in the
first person.

Examples of "gossip" in the content of the group multilogue
might be:

Joe: "Pete, I am mad at you now for doing those silly
things."

Bill: "Joe, I am mad at Pete, too."

Co-leader: "Bill, you are talking *about* Pete. Please talk
(Intervention)   directly to him."

Bill:	"Pete, I am mad at you too, and would like you to quit doing the things that you later regret."

———————

Mary:	"John didn't really mean what he said, I'm sure."
Co-leader: (Intervention)	"Mary, would you please speak directly to John."
Mary:	"John, I don't think that you really meant that comment to be destructive."

Blocking the There and Then

Co-leaders may need to continue their traffic directions in helping members focus on the here and now throughout the life of the group. Some participants seem able to learn quickly to exist in the present time and place. Others need direction from the co-leaders or members to relate their comments to the here and now of group life, intra- and interpersonal experiencing as it is currently happening within the group.

Some "there and then" content may be appropriate, but co-leaders will constantly monitor this content for current relevancy. What do a member's verbalizations mean to him right now? What is he saying to the group right now? What is he saying to another member right now? Interventions by the co-leaders will refocus mind sets on the immediate experiencing of members, away from reliving the past or rehearsing the future.

As members talk about the "there and then" world, they tend to talk in generalities, using "we," "people," "all of us," and "they," rather than take full responsibility for the comments by beginning their sentences with "I." Appealing to the authority of the majority is a common way people control one another. A co-leader must intervene in group so that members learn to indicate clearly their responsibility for their own statements. The prelude to taking responsibility is to recognize first those habitual speech patterns which shift authority to others. A representative dialogue may illustrate these points:

Sue:	"As a group we haven't helped each other at all."

Co-leader: (Intervention)	"It seems to me, Sue, that you can talk only for yourself, how you feel right now."
Sue:	"Okay. I don't feel that I have been helped by anyone here at all and I wish someone would help me."
Co-leader: (Intervention)	"Would you please be more specific. Maybe there is someone in particular you have in mind. . . ."
Sue:	"Yeah, you, John, and you, Jane, and you Pete— I wish each of you would give me something about what it is that might make people think I don't care about them."
Co-leader:	"Understanding, Sue, that John can only talk for himself, and Jane can only talk for herself and Pete can only talk for himself."
Pete:	"I would like to respond Sue. I . . . (etc.) "

Jim:	"Last week, during group, I really was shook up. . . ."
Co-leader:	"And apparently, still have some feelings about it right now. . . ."

Blocking Super-Mothering

"Super-mothering" is not restricted to the female sex. Males, as well as females, often intervene in confrontations in an effort to assuage hostility, guilts, and pain. The "s'mothering" is done in an apparent effort to be helpful. Actually it is highly manipulative. Probably few members recognize their interventions as motivated by their own inability to confront these emotions; that doing something for someone always has an element of manipulation in the act.

Very often in group one member is engaged in a confrontation with himself or with another member and another participant interjects a "soothing" comment. The intensity of the confrontation is at best lessened and may be diverted by the super-mothering behavior. A member may thus be denied the opportunity to face some intra- or interpersonal conflict which might be a source of growth for him. The co-leader will divert the super-mothering intervention so that the confrontation may be completed to resolution. The dialogue illustrates:

John:	"Jim, when you shake your finger at me like that, I get all tight inside."
Mary:	(To John) "Jim doesn't mean anything by it. He is just making a point."
Co-leader:	"Mary, your are denying John's feelings. John is saying something he wants Jim to hear."

or

Mae:	"I feel betrayed. I believed him and now I know he lied to me. I guess I'm partly angry because I see myself as being taken advantage of and made a fool of."
Mary:	"Well, Mae, we all have felt that way at times. I think everybody is made a fool of at one time or another. I remember once. . . ."

Blocking Mind-raping

One of the most difficult interventions to make is that of calling attention to the dynamic in which one participant makes assumptions about what another is thinking or feeling. The member who is thus "interpreted" is negated and illegitimatized. His mind is raped and very likely he is unaware of the process. As co-leaders perform their traffic-directing functions, they may bring into awareness that a rape has occurred.

Mind-raping may be confused with feedback. The difference is subtle, but in the former a participant is "reading" another's thoughts while in the latter the participant delivering feedback is taking full responsibility for his thoughts, and reactions.

An example of mind-raping:

Maria:	"I wish I could like you, Henry, but I always have a feeling of wanting to get away when I am with you."

66

Henry: (mind-raping)	"That is because you think I am judging you."
Co-leader:	"Henry, you are putting thoughts into Maria's mind, and throwing the responsibility onto her."
Henry:	"Okay, Maria, I guess I can't speak for what is in your mind, but when I am with you this is how I feel. I . . . etc."

A more subtle example:

Maria:	"When I am with you, Henry, I have a need to get away from you . . . I feel uneasy. . . ."
Henry: (mind-raping)	"Yeah you have uneasiness in the stomach, you have fears of being with me, you have unrecognized sexual responses, and really would like to confront me, but you can't."
Co-leader:	"Henry, you have put words to feelings that you only assume Maria has . . . I haven't heard how it is with Maria . . ."

Another example:

Maria:	"When I am with you Henry, I feel. . . ."
Henry: (mind-raping)	"Mm-hmm, uneasy, uptight, like you would not want to be there, anxious. . . ."
Co-leader:	"Henry, you interrupted Maria, and have not allowed her to finish how it is with her. . . ."

Blocking Invasion of Privacy

One of the major traffic-directing functions of the co-leaders is to protect the privacy of the members. Questions provide one speech pattern which results in privacy invasion. The technique of question-blocking has already been addressed in this chapter. Another area in which the co-leader will function as traffic director is to block content

67

which may invade privacy. In adult groups members can safely volunteer materials from their own life spaces and can exercise judgment as to what to bring to group and what they may wish to avoid. When a group consists of minors who are drawn from a public school setting the protection of privacy becomes more complex. Students *must* have their family's privacy protected as well as their own, and very often a young person will not have the judgment to know whether or not content is appropriate to bring to a group.

The co-leaders must be alert to any content which may damage the group members or their families, particularly in the public school setting. For example if a student group member who is a minor brings up his concern regarding his homosexuality, a co-leader would immediately block elaboration of the content. He cannot, obviously, prevent such material from being presented. He can avoid further discussion by focusing on other areas. A student group member may wish to describe a quarrel his mother and father had. This material should *not* be pursued; rather, the privacy of the mother and father must be protected. The co-leaders can focus on concerns and feelings members are experiencing in the here and now.

Privacy is one of the major content differences in individual and group counseling. The areas dealing with family relationships, deviant sexuality, and people not present are three content areas which are *not* appropriate in a group setting, but which are most appropriate for exploration in individual counseling. When these content areas come up in the group context, the co-leaders do not further the discussion, but as inconspicuously as possible suggest that the matter be discussed on a one-to-one basis. A general principle which should be followed is that the exploration or discussion of any content which may later damage a student or his family must not be encouraged in group. The counselor must and will deal with these areas in the privacy of the individual counseling relationship.

Example:

Sally: "My mother and father really got into it last night. He came home drunk as usual. . . ."

Co-counselor: "I am reacting right now, Sally, with some ten-
(Intervention) sion to your rapid speech and facial scowls. . . ."

68

Sally: "Yeah, I really feel uptight. I'm tense and I would kind of like to yell at all of you here."

Jim: "I'm kind of mixed up. I had a dream last night that I was in a show and a queer sat down next to me. I didn't know what to do."

Counselor: "Dreams are sometimes confusing, Jim. Why
(Intervention)   can't you and I get together later and talk about it."

MODELING

The interventions of the above dialogues combined the traffic-directing function, in which the counselor intervened to focus on the here and now in a participant's personal frame of reference, blocking family problems, sexual problems, and the there-and-then which dealt with individuals outside the group. In the examples the co-counselor's interventions also were performing the function of modeling. The co-counselor used himself as a model, verbalizing his own reactions to the speakers. He communicated to the group where he was, how he was feeling, what he was thinking, and, in the process, taking full responsibility for his own verbalizations.

When a co-counselor is performing the function of modeling, members may at times assume he is being another member. When a co-counselor transmits how it is with him, group members are not always aware and need not be aware that the purpose of the leader's transmission is to share himself so that he provides a model of authentic interaction. It is not necessary that members differentiate between these leadership-membership roles, but it is vital that the leader does.

The *modeling* function involves a co-counselor working in the framework of the extensional model, remaining in the here and now, avoiding use of questions, honoring and protecting the private life spaces of members, emphasizing positive elements rather than negative elements, being himself authentic and open, relating to members I-to-Thou, and transmitting a stance of "I'm okay, you're okay" (Harris, 1967). He also models the verbal vehicles which make group processes unique—confrontation and feedback. He "teaches" how to be a group member through his own modeling; he does not "teach" group membership by talking about it.

A dialogue illustrating modeling follows:

Joe:	"I like people very much and I want to be liked. I find it hard to talk to people I don't know."
Mary:	"I was wondering if you were ever going to talk, Joe."
Co-counselor:	"Joe, it really makes me feel good to have you enter into the group tonight. I like hearing about your feelings about members here."

Another example of modeling:

Gerry:	"I really react to you Ada, when you smile. It makes me feel warm and accepted."
Co-counselor:	"Yeah, I can relate to that, Gerry. I respond the same way, Ada. When you smile at me, I feel recognized and legitimatized and very much okay, and I like that."

INTERACTION CATALYST

Just as the modeling function overlaps the traffic-directing function, so does the modeling function overlap the interaction catalyst function. In order to activate group processes a co-leader does certain things for certain purposes. He serves as interaction catalyst so that the process begins to move; people get involved at a productive level; movement to confrontation is aided; values are examined; awareness of self is heightened.

A co-leader will usually serve as interaction catalyst at the beginning of a session. He uses, if necessary, some technique to help participants move from the work and social world into the unique world of group. This book provides an abundance of techniques designed to assist leaders in their catalytic function. As a group learns membership skills and responsibilities, a co-leader may not have to continue functioning as catalyst. Group members will soon be able to plunge into a working level without help, and at such times, of course, co-leaders model, traffic-direct, and aid communication, but do not need to catalyze interaction.

When a co-leader does choose to use an interaction catalyst technique, he may or may not choose to model that technique. A general guide is to keep in mind that the co-leader models only for the benefit of the group participants; thus if a technique needs to be demonstrated to be effective, a co-leader will begin, performing a modeling function. For example, if a co-leader wishes to activate interaction by using the technique of asking each member to find a concrete object in the immediate environment to which he can relate in a personal way, the co-leader will, in all likelihood, choose to begin the "go round" by modeling. He will present his object to the group, and try to communicate those elements of his essence which he sees the object representing. The other co-leader will invite feedback to the co-leader who has been modeling, then will begin the interaction in the group by asking for volunteers. If, at this point, no other member feels comfortable about volunteering, the second co-leader can model, using his object. After feedback has been generated to the second presentation, and no member volunteers, the co-leaders should remain silent until members pick up their responsibility to the group and begin interacting.

The reader is referred to material throughout this manual for examples of the interaction catalyst function of co-leaders; thus no dialogue has been presented at this point.

COMMUNICATION FACILITATOR

A final micro-function of group leadership which can be identified and learned is that of comunication facilitator. The functions of a leader as communication facilitator have been addressed in the preceding chapter, where the nature of the leader's techniques was presented. Additional facilitating behaviors are discussed here.

As communication facilitator of interaction and feedback, each co-leader will draw heavily on his individual counseling skills. Verbal responses which are effective when working in a one-to-one relationship also may be effective when working in the complex of the group relationship. Various modes of response which might be helpful to a group leader are described in the following paragraphs.

Reflecting Content

Much of the discussion which takes place in the group interaction needs a focus if members are to be aware of meanings and implications. The co-leader can reflect content, rephrasing material in fresh, new words, capturing the essence of the statements so that members can hear more accurately their own and others' verbalizations.

Avis: "You might not show it, basically right out. But deep down you may think you despise your parents and might tell everybody you hate them, but deep down you actually know you really love your parents. Kids under 18 have to have someone over them, and they actually are afraid of losing that, but they don't really know it."

Co-leader: "Afraid of losing the security of having someone responsible for you."

Avis: "Yes, all kids need someone to tell them what to do."

Co-leader: "You need to have someone to help you make decisions."

Linking

The process of tying one member's comments to another member's comments may at times be helpful. The linking response may either involve ideas or feelings, and perhaps may link verbal and non-verbal messages.

Jeanne:
(Smiling) "I really dislike my principal. He always comes creeping into my classroom when I least expect him."

Co-counselor: "I am confused by the two messages I am receiving—a smiling one from your face and tone of voice, and an angry one from your words."

Reflecting Feelings

Any counselor trained in a non-directive stance is adept at reflecting feelings. The response is difficult to learn, but once learned, becomes almost automatic. The danger of this verbal response pattern is that it can become trite and parrot-like, and thus insulting. A counselor must be sensitive in order to verbalize feelings accurately, and be careful not to mind-rape in the process.

Greg:	"I have an hour after I get home from school before I go to work, and the minute I walk in that house I get nagged at—nothing but complaints."
Co-leader:	"Right now feeling kind of angry. . . ."
Greg:	"You darn right. Nag! Nag! But why?"
Co-leader:	"Feelings of hopelessness. . . ."

The Ears of the Leaders

The *eyes* of the leaders constantly monitor nonverbal communications within the group; the *ears* of the leaders constantly monitor verbal communications; the processing of these processes constitutes the listening skills of a leader. He sees, he hears, he feels, he sorts, he discriminates, he reacts, he acts. The ears of the leaders are antennae which pick up not only surface content, but also meanings and implications which are not always apparent to the untrained listener. The listening-responding feedback role of group leaders *must* be based on a thorough working knowledge of personality theory. Background in the dynamics of human behavior must be a part of the professional preparation leaders bring to groups. The intent of the following comments is to identify possible areas of sensitive listening which might be processed by group leaders as they function in their role of facilitators. It is not the intent to provide a "listening cookbook" which can substitute for extensive background in psychological theory.

One major "listening post" for leaders who function in the Extensional model is the explicit and implicit value hierarchies of each member. A participant can extend his life space more effectively if he has an awareness of the value base from which he operates. One role of the leaders is to use their listening skills to help members "hear" their value systems. As members interact these systems are clearly

73

disclosed, and when appropriate, leaders can provide feedback. Obviously leaders avoid judgmental responses; the "goodness" or "badness" label attached to a value arises from a member; leaders neither approve nor disapprove. Their task is to help each member "hear" his own values and to become aware of his priorities. What an individual member does with this knowledge outside the group, is his responsibility. Adult participants, through their verbal and nonverbal expressions, will indicate that they have internalized stances toward the traditional cultural values of work, achievement, "things," friends, cleanliness, honesty, learning, thrift, travel, and so forth, but may be only dimly aware of how these stances have been translated into a unique life style (individuation). Preadolescent and adolescent participants, through verbal and nonverbal expressions, may indicate their questioning of traditional cultural value systems, but, as they examine their own values, may find that they are chiefly "reactive" rather than "proactive," i.e., *against* something rather than *for* something. For example, the value of nonconformity requires that there be a conformity against which to be non-conforming. Group leaders use *their* listening skills to help participants identify their existent value systems and become aware of implications for life styles.

Leaders listen, too, to life-space verbalizations concerning areas which members may choose to change. For example, leaders may wish to take particular note of expressions of inadequacy, incompetency, worthlessness, despair, expressions of "I'm not okay," etc. These negative self-expressions probably represent changes participants would like to make in their personality functioning. Comments concerning feelings of rejection of others or self, of wishes to "get even" or to be punished—in general, of deficiency needs—may point to areas members will want to examine. Verbalizations concerning guilt feelings, feelings of loneliness, of isolation, of depression may be possible indicators that a "human nourishment" deficiency exists, and perhaps group would be the source where this deficency is relieved.

We would like to emphasize again that leaders may or may not respond verbally to the content they "hear." They may only make mental notes of overt or covert expressions of a member's ambivalent, conflicted feelings about a significant other. A leader may only silently

74

monitor expressions of members' neurotic needs to control others, to possess others, to manipulate others, etc. In the Extensional model he is more likely to respond verbally to non-neurotic needs of creativity, self-expression, and enjoyment. In general, in this model leaders will process both deficiency and growth needs but may respond verbally more frequently to the latter.

A thorough knowledge of defense mechanisms seems essential for group leaders as they take note of characteristic defense modes of members. Rationalizations, projections, intellectualizations, denials, etc. may be data which a leader might process, but not verbalize. The current developmental task which each member is addressing, however, probably will be identified to bring it into the member's awareness so that he can more actively cope with it.

The ears of the leader are acutely tuned to grammatical and speech-pattern cues to understanding a member's life space. If a leader is to be of use to a member in extending his functioning, then the leader must understand that life space. One way to do so is to pick up speech cues. In the writers' experience any statement beginning with "I" is important. "My," "mine," "ours,"—any possessive, probably— should be filed. "Shoulds" and "oughts" are significant other-directed speech patterns. Any statement qualified by "but," any statement seeking approval, such as "okay?," excessive verbiage, excessive questioning, sighs, excessive explainings, apologies, speech intonations and hesitancies, demanding, commanding, doubting, contradicting— all represent verbal cues which a leader processes so that he can enter fully into the life space of a member. The intent is not to violate life space, but to use professional skills to extend a member's life space.

Communication Patterns to Avoid

Certain speech behaviors are not helpful in communication in group. Questioning has already been discussed as basically hostile and a way of controlling others. Interpreting is a form of mind-raping which is avoided in the Extensional model. Calling attention to the group process is also not helpful as this tends to make an object out of the group and thus of group members; therefore, the writers suggest that leaders avoid talking about the process itself with the group except when training leaders. Summarizing is also seldom helpful. This speech pattern places a period on communication which may inhibit growth. Rather than summarizing, it is recommended that group leaders routinely "cap" at the end of each session. The technique of capping is addressed at length elsewhere in this manual (p. 57). Speech patterns of "I hear you saying . . ." are irritating and usually represent mind-raping. Sentences begun with "You feel . . . ," "You are feeling . . . ," are patronizing and also represent mind-raping. Any efforts to elicit a "because" answer or an answer to a "why" are not helpful. Shoulds and should nots, "don't worry," "I was there, too," "I understand how you feel because . . . ," "I coped with it, so you can . . ." are all speech patterns which must be avoided by group leaders. Members may exhibit these verbal behaviors, but leaders need not. A straight comment, a clear position, a risk of self, and an I-to-Thou verbalization are helpful, and as a leader functions as communication faciiltator he will model these speech patterns.

SUMMARY

The four micro-functions of group leadership have been addressed in this chapter: traffic-directing, modeling, interaction catalyst, and communication facilitator. As was pointed out in the introductory remarks, these functions at times overlap and interweave and at times are discrete. As leaders develop these components of leadership they will soon learn to perform them smoothly and intuitively.

CHAPTER 5

CONTROLS FOR THE GROUP PROCESSES
—COGNITIVE MAPS

- The Johari Window
- The Hill Interaction Matrix
- Bibliography

To the Group Leader:

This chapter presents your intellectual tools—the cognitive maps you need to function as group leader.

CHAPTER 5

CONTROLS FOR THE GROUP PROCESSES
—COGNITIVE MAPS

The thought of control is repugnant to group leaders, and the suggestion of manipulation is equally distasteful. Thus, when the recommendation is made that through their functions of traffic directing, modeling, catalyst and facilitation, group leaders both control and manipulate group processes, the initial reaction is one of horror. Yet, that is exactly what group leaders must do—control and manipulate the *processes* of group interaction; they never, under any circumstances, attempt to control and manipulate the *participants*.

Once the necessity for controlling and manipulating the group processes is recognized as a responsibility of group leadership, the need arises for leadership tools which can be used to accomplish these ends. These are in addition to the theoretical framework from which Extensional group leaders operate and which is discussed elsewhere in this volume. The tools which are the focus of these comments are cognitive maps of the group processes—"The Johari Window" (Luft and Ingham, 1963) , and the *Hill Interaction Matrix* (Idem) .

THE JOHARI WINDOW

The Johari Window provides the group leader and members with a cognitive map which sets direction of the group processes. The exotic title of the Window comes from a combination of the first names of the two men who put the original model together—Joseph Luft and Harry Ingham—hence, Joe-Hari. The original model delineated the relationship of one person (represented by the four cells) to others. The following adaptation of Luft and Ingham's conceptual scheme is suggested as a means of ordering the group processes and content into a simple cognitive map which provides direction for both leaders and members. It is suggested that the leaders present the general idea of the window as outlined below in an orientation session, so as to give all potential participants a road map of the group process which they can follow as well as an understanding of their responsibilities as group members. At this point the leaders also, through the Window, are clarifying the safeguards to privacy which they will provide to participants. Figure 5-1 is an adaptation of the Johari Window to the Extensional group model. The following comments discuss

FIGURE 5-1

A COGNITIVE MAP OF GROUP PROCESSES
(ADAPTED FOR GROUPS FROM THE JOHARI WINDOW*)

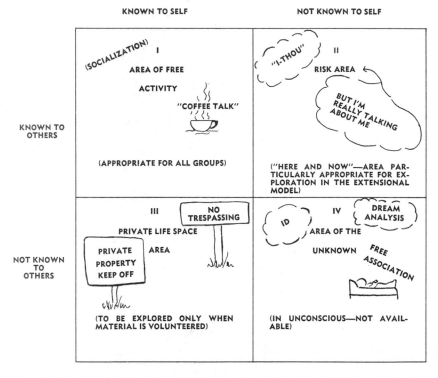

*Originally formulated by Joseph Luft and Harry Ingham in "The Johari Window, A Graphic Model of Awareness in Interpersonal Relations." pp. 10-12, in *Group Processes: An Introduction to Group Dynamics* by Joseph Luft, Palo Alto: National Press Books, 1963.

the Window as it applies to this group model and are presented in the order suggested for the orientation session.

Johari Window Cell I: Area of Free Activity
Known to me— Known to you

The first cell of the window represents content which is known to me about me and is readily available or is known to others. This content is the fabric of social intercourse around which we build our daily interchanges, e.g., we all know that the writers of this manual are interested in groups; we all know that we write, and so forth. Out of this knowledge, known to me about me and known to you about me, can be built a commonality of interest which may lead to friendship. It is this content area which we routinely use in social situations to build and to perpetuate relationships.

We operate in this cell as we interface daily with one another. As we expand the size of Cell I, we come to know more and more about each other, and may come to care more and more for each other. The content material of this cell will be primarily cognitive, although it may contain some conative content. The prime characteristic of the content in this cell is that it is typical of material we deal with in our routine activities. Therefore, while it is useful as a vehicle around which to build group communication and group acquaintanceship, interaction in this cell is *not* unique to a group, but may be obtained in a variety of circumstances.

Johari Window Cell IV: Area of the Unknown
Unknown to me—Unknown to you

Cell IV represents material which by definition is unavailable—the unconscious. I do not know what resides in my unconscious nor do you know what resides there. It may be brought into awareness through hypnosis, or free association, or dream analysis, but without special efforts the material remains below the level of awareness. The exploration of this cell in the usual interaction group is not appropriate. For the leader to deal with these kinds of materials requires a high degree of skill and training, and thus the cell is "off limits" for counseling groups.

Johari Window Cell III: Private Life Space Area
Known to me—Not known to you

Cell III represents the area which is most often violated in the name of the group process. Destructive group experiences usually center in this cell. Travesties mislabeled "group encounters" and "sensitivity groups" center in this cell. If groups tend to be perceived as a negative force, it is probably because the perceiver conceptualizes groups as operating from this cell. If a person has experienced group as negative, it may well be that the leader and members probed into the private life spaces represented by this cell, violating a member's human dignity.

This cell represents the body of knowledge each of us knows about ourselves but which we do not know about each other. This concerns our private, personal lives. If, in a group, members or leader intrude into that private, personal area, they have trespassed into another's life space. No one in a group is welcome to solicit through questioning or any other means material from Area III. When a member *volunteers* content from his private, personal life space, then and only then is it available to the group. Until that time the "No Trespassing" sign must be observed.

Group leaders have the responsibility of protecting the Cell III area of each member; the traffic-directing function is directed toward this end. A leader does not allow members to probe into private areas of one another's lives. He does not allow one member to volunteer another member's Cell III material. He is constantly alert that no one does so, nor does he do so himself. He makes it clear that members feel comfortable in saying, "I do not wish to discuss that" without being labeled as "Bad Group Members" or accused of having a "hangup" about something. The astute leader will recognize that Cell III is where Groupsmen practice their merry games, all in the name of an "honesty" which could be more accurately described as "psychological infiltration."

A group member may choose to deal in the group with concerns he has from Cell III of his life space and may bring these concerns to the group where they can be discussed. The material, however, must directly concern him and not others close to him. Participants in interaction groups sometimes wrongly introduce material which concerns the Cell III life space of their significant others, considering it appropriate for them to bring to the group. For example, a member might relate how his wife is a sloppy housekeeper and cannot manage their money. The alert group leader will immediately realize that the member is intruding into the Cell III life space of his wife, and as a leader will suggest that the group member deal with *his* feelings about the situation, not his wife's behaviors. The focus thus is maintained on the existent experience in the here-and-now of the group member, not on the past or present experience in the there-and-then—in this instance, a wife's housekeeping behaviors.

It is from Cell III material that the issue of confidentiality usually arises. In some groups members are requested to keep all material discussed in the group confidential; it is content derived from this cell which will be at issue. While a group leader certainly does not want to discourage members from exploring concerns they have from their own Cell III, he does take the risk of confidentiality being violated each time material is introduced from this area. In the public school setting, involving students, it is particularly important that material from Cell III be handled very cautiously, for the school group counselor has no way at all of guaranteeing confidentiality on behalf of student group members, only himself. Thus his only recourse is to discourage exploration among members of material from Cell III which will violate the privacy of a member's family. If a student wishes to discuss a family argument the leader blocks content description and will assist the member in dealing with his here and now feelings and behaviors in the group; then, if necessary, see the student privately.

Johari Window Cell II: Risk Area, The Group Arena
Not known to me—Known to you

If a leader takes the position that Cell I is useful— but *not* unique —to groups and is available in a variety of settings; that Cell IV is by definition not available; that Cell III invades privacy and may only be volunteered by an individual member concerning himself, then what areas can be tapped so that the group process is productive? The answer lies in Cell II. Here can be found that material which is unique to groups and, in normal human interface, not tapped. The properties of Cell II are described below.

Group Leadership

There is a body of material which is known to *you* about me and which *I* do not know about me; which is known to *me* about you and which *you* do not know about you. This concerns how I am experiencing you and how you are experiencing me. You, and *only* you, are the sole source of information regarding how you are reacting to me, and I have no way of obtaining these data until you are willing to give them to me. Conversely, I, and only I, am the sole source of information regarding how I am reacting to you, and you have no way of obtaining these data until I give them to you.

If the uniqueness of the group process is to be tapped, I must be willing to give you feedback out of this risk area. As I communicate with you concerning my responses to you, it must be understood that there will be no implication that you should change. You may or may not choose to do so. If a number of the group members experience the same reaction, you may give the feedback more weight, but, on the other hand, you may choose only to recognize their statements as useful information to be filed.

Cell II will tap solely the here and now of the group process—how one member is experiencing another in that existent moment. Content will not deal with life outside the group, but with what is going on within the group. Confidentiality thus does not become an issue. Members can use the group process in the way it is unique—that of an arena in which honest, genuine, uncensored feedback is given "I to Thou." There may be negative reactions expressed, but there will probably be as many, if not more, positive reactions expressed. The interaction which takes place is at a level of intense experiencing together of each passing moment and the experiencing is described verbally. The functions of modeling, facilitating, and catalyst all have as their purpose to maintain the intensity of Cell II material.

There are few situations outside a group where such interactions are appropriate. If, in routine social intercourse, people were to describe their ongoing reaction to each other at this level of intensity, it is probable that economic productivity would be diminished. Frequent bulletins from "viscera land" become ludicrous, and, unless all concerned are operating from Cell II agendas, the misunderstandings which occur are infinite—and disastrous. "In" group is another matter.

The interaction group is unique in that here, and usually only here,

84

is the total agenda for each of us to obtain honest feedback on how others are experiencing us. This requires that members of a group risk themselves to perform this "act of grace." When a member responds to another out of Cell II he is giving a part of himself not usually offered. He is risking rejection and misunderstanding; he is lowering his defenses, and becomes open and vulnerable. Thus, this kind of feedback represents a gift of great value—an act of grace, something of infinite worth—a part of another human being.

This act of grace—giving authentic feedback and receiving the gift of honest reaction—is built on a principle which *must* be transmitted to the group by the leader and which will need to be reinforced throughout the life of the group. (The obvious application to life outside the group requires no comment.) This principle is basic to this area of communication: "When I speak, I speak only about me, about my values, about what I feel is good or bad for me. My feedback to you is a statement about me. If I react to you in an assertive or attacking manner, or if I relate to you in a neutral or nonrisking monologue, or if I relate to you in a caring, empathic way, I am communicating how it is with me and I am risking something of my essence."

It is the group leader's responsibility as one of his traffic-directing functions to keep this basic principle surfaced in the group processes: that every statement we make, in the final analysis, is about ourselves. For example, if I say "You are stupid," the statement carries no credence concerning your character nor should it be internalized by you as a reality about *you*. Rather, when I make this assertion of your being stupid, I am speaking from *my* biases, and *my* emotional sets. What I really am saying is that *I* am experiencing frustrations, dislikes of your behavior, and am unable to cope with you at this time. Thus the "you are stupid" statement is really a statement about *me*—not about you; not that I am stupid, but that I see what you are doing as stupid. If you choose to internalize my comments as belonging to you rather than to me, this would diminish both of us. You will have given over your autonomy and I will have been experienced as judger. Rather, in feedback, you might choose to legitimatize my feelings as a truth about me—that I am perceiving your behaviors as stupid—and our dialogue can continue, with the channels of communication wide open.

Buddha recognized this truth long before the Extensional group existed—that when a person speaks he only speaks of and for himself. A parable tells the story of a foolish man who, learning that Buddha observed the principle of returning good for evil, came and abused him. Buddha was silent until the man finished, then asked, "If I decline to accept a gift made to me, to whom then does the gift belong?" The man answered, "In that case, it would still belong to the man who offered it." Buddha replied, "Since I decline to accept your abuse, does it not then belong to you?" The man made no reply but walked slowly away, carrying with him that which he had wished to give to another (Siu, 1968).

THE HILL INTERACTION MATRIX

The Johari Window provides a general cognitive map which can give direction to both leaders and members. While the Window provides some guidelines for group interaction, it does not provide a group leader with a tool through which he has command of the group processes. Again, it should be emphasized that the leader must be in control of the group—the safety of group members depends on the leader's technical skills. To control the process, however, does *not* imply that leaders control members.

The cognitive map which provides leaders with a sophisticated tool to control the group process is found in the *Hill Interaction Matrix* (HIM) (See Figure 5-2). While the HIM was developed for use with therapy patients and for groups outside the school setting, it is applicable to Extensional groups of all age levels. The HIM is useful in two ways:

1. It gives a reference point to conceptualize the general areas where various theoretical orientations tend to focus, e.g., the non-directive and the behavioral groups are likely to have a tendency to operate at the conventional level of interaction until a leader takes action, while a psychoanalytical group will operate in the main at a speculative level. The group which is conceived within the Existentialist framework, the Extensional model, will tend to function at the confrontive level. (An identification of the areas on the HIM where various models of groups tend to operate can be found in Figure 5-3.)

2. It provides a cognitive map by which leaders can maintain con-

FIGURE 5-2

HILL INTERACTION MATRIX*

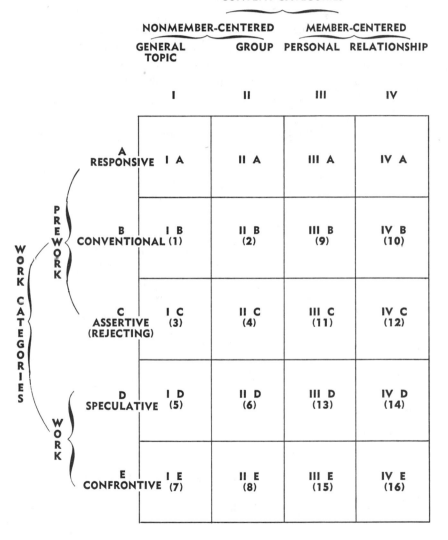

CONTENT CATEGORIES

NONMEMBER-CENTERED   MEMBER-CENTERED

GENERAL   GROUP   PERSONAL RELATIONSHIP
TOPIC

	I	II	III	IV
A RESPONSIVE	I A	II A	III A	IV A
B CONVENTIONAL	I B (1)	II B (2)	III B (9)	IV B (10)
C ASSERTIVE (REJECTING)	I C (3)	II C (4)	III C (11)	IV C (12)
D SPECULATIVE	I D (5)	II D (6)	III D (13)	IV D (14)
E CONFRONTIVE	I E (7)	II E (8)	III E (15)	IV E (16)

WORK CATEGORIES

PREWORK

WORK

*Developed by Dr. Ida Coppolino and Dr. W. F. Hill (Copies of the booklets describing the development and scoring of the *Matrix* are available from W. Hill, Youth Studies Center, University of Southern California, Los Angeles).

trol of the group process, a map which provides direction for modeling, facilitating, and stimulating interaction through catalytic techniques. The various categories of the HIM should be mastered by group leaders who may or may not elect to teach them to members. Once leaders clearly identify levels of interaction of group content, they can easily model and facilitate communication at whatever level they wish. Whether or not it is useful for members to be aware of this cognitive map will be a professional decision that individual leaders must make. Figures 5-4 and 5-5 present representative comments which illustrate interaction levels on the *Matrix*. Figure 5-4 presents comments taken from an adolescent group and Figure 5-5 presents comments made by an adult group.

Content Categories

The HIM is divided into four categories of content, two of which are *nonmember*-centered and two of which are *member*-centered. The nonmember-centered content category is divided into two types— (1) content dealing with general *topics* which are appropriate in common social intercourse, and (2) content which deals with the *group process* itself. For example, a comment might be made, "Juvenile delinquency sure seems to be increasing," or "What type of group seems to be most productive?" Leaders might allow the comment to generate reaction at the stimulus level (i.e., Conventional-General and Conventional-Group) or they might choose to respond to attitudes behind the surface comment and move to Confrontive or Speculative levels.

FIGURE 5-3
THEORETICAL MODELS: TYPICAL AREA OF OPERATION ON THE HIM

MATRIX LEVELS	THEORIES	CELLS
RESPONSIVE	TO BE USED WITH REGRESSED PATIENTS IN MENTAL INSTITUTIONS	
CONVENTIONAL	PHENOMENOLOGICAL (NON-DIRECTIVE)	IB, IIB, IIIB, IVB
	BEHAVIORAL	IB, IIB, IIIB, IVB
	GESTALT	IB, IIB, IIIB, IIIE
ASSERTIVE	SYNANON GAMES	IIC, IIIC, IVC
SPECULATIVE	PSYCHOANALYTICAL	ID, IID, IIID, IVD
CONFRONTIVE	EXISTENTIALIST EXTENSIONAL	III E & IVE

Member-centered content can be subdivided into content which deals with a member's personal world or content which deals with the relationship between two or more members of the group. For example, a group member might comment, "I sure had a good time at the party last night," which would represent a Conventional-Personal comment; or he might say, "I am certainly interested in your point of view, Jean. Go on, and explain more" (Conventional-Relationship).

The HIM, then, orders content within a group into that which is nonmember-centered and that which is member-centered. Both are seen as facilitating self-understanding—the nonmember-centered indirectly and the member-centered directly. The nonmember-centered content may concern topics of general interest or it may concern the group process itself. Member-centered may focus on a member's personal life space or it may focus on the relationship of members of the group with each other.

The relative productivity of each cell is measured by the weight given below each cell designation in Figure 5-2, i.e., 1-16. Thus, Cell IB (Conventional-Topic) has a minimum productivity value of "1" while Cell IVE (Confrontive-Relationship) has a maximum productivity value of "16" (Hill, idem).

Work Categories

The HIM divides possible *content* material of groups into the four categories enumerated above (I, II, III, and IV). The *Matrix* also orders possible *levels* of interaction into two *Work Categories: Prework* and *Work*. These are designated by capital letters A, B, C, D, and E.

The Prework categories are labeled Responsive, Conventional, and Assertive, while the work categories are Speculative and Confrontive (See Figure 5-2). Each prework and work level will be discussed in order, beginning with the Responsive category.

The *Responsive* level of the HIM is not relevant to the type of groups which are the focus of this book. The HIM uses the Responsive category to designate those comments elicited by a therapist from hospitalized psychiatric patients. This restricted category is utilized in the main with regressed or retarded patients, and the therapeutic objective is to motivate patients to interact and become social beings —that is, capable of operating at the conventional level.

Conventional content serves the function of maintaining socialization within a group. It also serves as an area to which a leader may direct interaction if he feels it appropriate at a given time, such as when he wishes to "cap," i.e., prepare members at the end of a session for re-entry into the nongroup world, the world of reality. It is important that a leader be aware that interaction at the conventional level may be either verbal or nonverbal (e.g., handshaking) and that, while conventional-level interaction is useful and necessary, it does not move from Cell I of the Johari window and is the type of interaction which can be experienced routinely outside the group.

Assertive behavior is so labeled as content in these cells signifies an assertion of self which represents a rejection of others and, perhaps, of the group process. It is prework. Members who demonstrate assertive behavior are saying, "I don't want to be involved, I don't want to work, I do not want to relate to you, etc., etc., etc." It is important that a leader recognize accurately such behavior for what it is. Members may seem to be working at confrontation while in reality they are "acting out." A member who states, "This group bores me," is making an assertive statement. He has rejected the process, does not recognize a concern on which he wishes to work, and does not provide members with content to which they can respond. Questions often are assertive and it is important that a leader be sensitive to the "hook" which is in assertive questions. He should, as he directs traffic, consistently insist that members verbalize the "hidden" assumptions which are behind every question, asking the questioner to make his position clear concerning the content of his question. For example, a group member may say to another group member who has just spoken, "Why did you say it that way?" The obvious hooks in the question are: (1) "I don't like the way you said it," (2) "I think your behavior is wrong," and (3) "I don't like you for saying that."

Attacking comments on the part of a group leader or members frequently are assertive rather than confrontive remarks. Such behavior can be entertaining (except for the "victim") and may provide a sexually stimulating evening. The excitement generated by acting out behavior may divert a leader's attention from the fact that it is prework and at a low level of productivity. Assertion remarks may

90

concern a general topic, the group itself, a rejection of self, or rejection of a relationship. A leader may or may not choose to deal with the meaning behind the rejection inherent in assertive behavior, but he must be aware of the dynamics behind such comments. (Figures 5-4 and 5-5 present representative comments which a reader may wish to study.)

The *Speculative* level of the HIM represents the first of the two work levels which operate in a group. Members who interact here have recognized a concern as centering in themselves and are willing to get down to work. At the speculative level members are not seeking ways to get others to change, but have recognized an area in themselves with which they wish to deal. They will be speculating about causes of behavior. The "I wonder why I'm this way" comment will be characteristic of this level of interaction as members seek explanations of current and previous actions. The level can be productive, but much historical "there and then" data will likely be verbalized, e.g., early rejection experiences. Members of the group who are skilled in playing the therapeutic game, (i.e., focus on examining *causes* of behaviors, rather than exploring alternatives for action) tend to remain on the speculative level unless leaders use catalytic techniques to move to confrontation.

Psychonanalytic groups tend to spend much time conjecturing in the speculative mode, posing many "why" questions, and groups can become seriously bogged down attempting to deal with irrelevant and unanswerable "why" questions when they might more productively be interacting in a here-and-now, I-Thou Extensional model. Again, it is also important for a group leader to recognize the hooks in questions and if he responds to the hook rather than traffic-directs the questioner to make a statement concerning his position, it is very likely that an academic debate will ensue and the group will be functioning in the conventional-topic (II A) cell of the matrix.

Confrontive. Where the conventional level is generally the area in which a non-directive group will function, and where the speculative level is generally the area in which a psychoanalytic group will operate, the Confrontive level is the *sine qua non* of an Extensional group. The focus will be on the "here and now," "I and Thou," rather than on the "I wonder whys?" of the speculative mode or the "Why don't *they*?" of the conventional mode.

FIGURE 5-4

TYPICAL STUDENT COMMENTS

	NONMEMBER-CENTERED		PERSONAL MEMBER-CENTERED	
	GENERAL TOPIC	GROUP	PERSONAL	RELATIONSHIP
	I	II	III	IV
Conventional	I PAID $6 TO HAVE MY HAIR STYLED & LOOK AT IT; IT LOOKS MUCH BETTER.	CAN'T WE GO FOR ANOTHER PERIOD. WE ARE JUST GETTING STARTED.	I ASKED DAD IF HE WANTED ME TO SMOKE BEHIND HIS BACK OR IN FRONT OF HIM AND HE SAID HE DIDN'T WANT ME TO SMOKE AT ALL.	I SEEM TO AGREE WITH YOU MOST OF THE TIME—LIKE WHEN YOU BELIEVE THAT GIRLS SHOULD NOT FIGHT . . . , EVEN WHEN THEY ARE CALLED NAMES.
Assertive	THE ONLY REASON KIDS DRINK IS TO THINK THEY'RE BIG.	I JUST LIKE TO LISTEN TO OTHERS TALK. IT MAKES ME NERVOUS TO TALK IN A GROUP.	WELL I'M PROUD OF IT. THE DUMB COP BELIEVED ME SO I MUST HAVE MADE IT GOOD AND I DIDN'T HAVE TO PAY, DID I.	SHUT UP! YOU THINK YOU KNOW EVERYTHING AND YOU DON'T. YOU CAN'T SMOKE ON A SCHOOL CAMPUS.
Speculative	I DON'T SEE WHY ADULTS HAVE THE RIGHT TO JUMP TO CONCLUSIONS ABOUT KIDS, & I DON'T SEE WHY THEY THINK THEY HAVE THE RIGHT TO CHOP US IN FRONT OF CLASS.	I WISH ALL OF US WOULD SAY WHAT WE THINK. I WONDER WHY WE DON'T.	I GUESS I DON'T HAVE A CONSCIENCE. I DIDN'T EVEN THINK HOW SHE WOULD FEEL WHEN I RAN AWAY.	I GUESS I DON'T LISTEN TO YOU BECAUSE YOU ALWAYS SEEM TO TRY TO USE ALL THOSE BIG WORDS I DON'T UNDERSTAND.
Confrontive	DEEP DOWN YOU MAY THINK YOU DESPISE YOUR PARENTS . . . , BUT DEEP DOWN YOU ACTUALLY KNOW YOU REALLY LOVE THEM!	WHY DOESN'T THE GROUP HELP ME WHEN I TALK.	IF I BORROW A DIME I DON'T EXPECT TO PAY IT BACK, BUT A DOLLAR IS DIFFERENT.	I THINK YOU ARE A LEECH. YOU BORROW MONEY AND DON'T PAY IT BACK AND MAKE A BIG JOKE OUT OF EVERTHING.

FIGURE 5-5

TYPICAL ADULT COMMENTS*

TOPIC	NONMEMBER-CENTERED GROUP	PERSONAL MEMBER-CENTERED	RELATIONSHIP MEMBER-CENTERED
I	II	III	IV
Conventional IT'S SURE COLD OUT TODAY.	WE HAVE NEW CHAIRS TODAY.	I LIKE TO COOK FOR MY FAMILY. I ENJOY IT.	YOU AND I REALLY SEEM TO HAVE A LOT IN COMMON, JIM.
Assertive AREN'T THOSE HIPPIES AWFUL? THEY ARE SO DIRTY!	THIS GROUP BORES ME! WE TALK AND TALK AND NEVER GET ANYWHERE.	I JUST WANT TO LISTEN. DON'T WORRY ABOUT ME.	YOU DON'T REALLY CARE ABOUT ME—YOU'RE JUST PRETENDING TO CARE.
Speculative I WONDER IF EVERYONE ISN'T NEUROTIC IN SOME WAY?	I WONDER WHY SOME MEMBERS TALK MORE THAN OTHERS?	WHY AM I SO SCARED TO SPEAK UP?	I GUESS I REACT TO YOU AS I WOULD TO MY MOTHER.
Confrontive MAYBE WE ALL HAVE A MOTHER AND FATHER IN US WHICH HAS TO BE SOMEHOW DONE AWAY WITH.	IN THE GROUP THE GIRLS ALL SIT ON ONE SIDE AND THE FELLOWS ON ANOTHER.	I KNOW I AM REACTING AS I THINK MY FATHER WOULD WANT AND I HATE MYSELF FOR IT BECAUSE IT ISN'T ME.	I REALLY TURN OFF WHEN YOU SHAKE YOUR FINGER AT ME — I WISH YOU WOULDN'T DO THAT.

*Reference: HIM Scoring Manual, *Wm. F. Hill, Youth Studies Center,*
U.S.C., Los Angeles.

The confrontive level requires a certain amount of ego strength on the part of the participants, and it is most essential—if this level of interaction is to remain healthy—that members internalize thoroughly the concept that they never really say anything about others but, in every statement he makes, each participant is essentially talking through his own system, with all his biases distorting reality, and responding through his own reactive and interactive being.

The speculative mode involves speculating on causes. The confrontive mode involves exploring how it is with you and how it is with me (Personal Confrontive) and how it is with-you-with-me. Some element of the unknown and perhaps some hostility may be present. Certainly the uniqueness that can be group interaction is most clear when members are working at confrontation. Seldom in normal social intercourse is it appropriate to interact at this level. The Risk Area (Cell II of the Johari Window) taps this area. Avoidance of this content will result in losing one of the most helpful dimensions of the group process.

George Bach (1967), in studying the dynamics of marathon groups, was able to identify dimensions of the group process which were helpful and dimensions which were blocking growth. Bach's findings can be applied to any interaction group and fit elegantly into the HIM. All five of the most helpful ways of interacting in groups fall at the confrontive level: (1) empathic identification, (2) acceptance-warmth, and (3) conflict acceptance all fall into Cell IVE-Confrontive-Relationship; (4) self-understanding and (5) problem-solving would be in the Personal-Confrontive Cell (Cell IIIE).

Bach's (ibid.) least helpful modes of interaction: (1) Strangeness, (2) Non-caring indifference, (3) Narcissism, (4) Irrelevant communication, and (5) Conflict evasion would all fall into the Assertive level of HIM.

Bach's studies confirm Hill's (1965) position that the Confrontive-Personal and Confrontive-Relationship cells of the HIM are the more productive areas for a member's growth. Thus, the group leader who is skilled enough in group processes to control levels of interaction can use the *Hill Interaction Matrix* as a sophisticated cognitive map which gives direction and focus to his leadership.

94

BIBLIOGRAPHY

Bach, George R. "Marathon Group Dynamics: Dimensions of Helpfulness: Therapeutic Aggression." *Psychological Reports,* 20, Southern Universities Press, 1967, pp. 1147-1158.

Bach, George R. "Marathon Group Dynamics: Disjunctive Contacts." *Psychological Reports,* 20, Southern Universities Press, 1967, pp. 1163-1172.

Bates, Marilyn, and Johnson, C. D. "The Existentialist Counselor at Work." *School Counselor,* March, 1969, pp. 245-250.

Hill, Wm. Fawcett, *Hill Interaction Matrix.* Los Angeles: Youth Studies Center, University of Southern California, 1965.

Hill, Wm. Fawcett. "The Hill Interaction Matrix." *Personnel and Guidance Journal,* April 1971, Vol. 49, #8, pp. 619-622.

Luft, Joseph. *Of Human Interaction.* Palo Alto, Ca.: National Press Books, 1969.

Luft, Joseph, and Ingham H. "The Johari Window: A Graphic Model of Awareness in Interpersonal Relations." *Group Processes: An Introduction to Group Dynamics.* Palo Alto: National Press Books, 1969, pp. 10-12.

Siu, R. G. H., *The Man of Many Qualities—A Legacy of the I. Ching.* Cambridge, Mass.: MIT Press, 1968, p. 73.

CHAPTER 6

TOOLS FOR GROUP INDUCTION

- Uniqueness of Groups
- Teaching Group Membership
- Pamphlet for Students
- Open Letter
- The Pre-Group Interview
- The Post-Group Interview
- Bibliography

To the Group Leader:

Group is unique and "how to be" a member must be taught—by you!

CHAPTER 6

TOOLS FOR GROUP INDUCTION

Group leaders ought not anticipate that group members know group process skills. There are no experiences in most of our lives which even begin to approach the group experience. The skills required to interact quickly and productively in the uniqueness which is group are quite different from the skills which keep social interactions comfortable. Polite consideration for another's feelings is essential in social intercourse. Censoring feelings and reactions may be most appropriate in employment situations. Without basic good manners we could not live and work together in harmony; and it is naive to assume that authenticity implies sharing promiscuously one's ongoing stream of visceral reactions. We do and must make a presentation of self in ordinary interactions which reflect only a portion of our multi-level selves—cognitive, conative, and sensual; conscious, preconscious, and unconscious—or only a portion of our multi-roles —worker, parent, offspring, companion, lover, friend. All our social roles require some censoring in our presentation of self if we are to remain functional (Note "Area of Free Activity" on Johari Window).

Group is something else again. Here suddenly, as leaders, we are asking participants to forego their normal social habits essential outside the group. We ask members to attempt temporarily to give up customary politeness and good manners, to refrain from censoring, and to respond to other group members with multi-level presentation of self. We ask members to report their feelings, their thoughts, and their spontaneous reactions to each other freely and fully without being concerned about the usual social rules of politeness and appropriateness. We ask members to interact with each other at levels which would be awkward if maintained consistently in the world outside the group.

UNIQUENESS OF GROUPS

This quality of uncensored interaction among group members represents the unique characteristics of the group process. There is not and never has been another situation in living which parallels group—this is true historically as well as cross-culturally. Nowhere in history has it been recorded that people anywhere have gathered together to share with each other as completely as possible their uncensored reactions to one another so that each may experience growth that will carry over to life outside the group. Thus, to expect that members will know how to use the process is unrealistic. The group leader must take the responsibility of inducting his members into ways of using the uniqueness that can be group. It is possible that through trial and error members will discover how to use a group, but this delays productive interaction while members are casting about trying to find their way.

'TEACHING' GROUP MEMBERSHIP

It is clearly a function of group leaders to "teach" group members to use the process and to transmit to group members an understanding of the unique characteristics of group membership. This involves presenting members with a cognitive understanding of the process, specifying their responsibilities as group members, and providing experiences of existing with a group. A feedback loop is thereby created which causes members to learn *about* the group process and come to an awareness of their responsibilities as participants as they are experiencing the process itself.

Leaders need two tools beyond the group process itself to activate the feedback loop: a cognitive map they can give to members to facilitate an understanding of the process, and a tool to communicate the responsibilities of group membership to potential members. The cognitive map recommended is the Johari Window which is presented elsewhere in this volume. The tools which are suggested to give members an understanding of their responsibilities of group membership differ according to age level. For students in public schools the pamphlet entitled *So You Are Going To Be In Group Counseling* (Appendix E) should be duplicated and placed in the hands of students at the time of the pre-group interview. Group leaders who

100

work in other institutional settings may wish to edit the pamphlet so as to make it appropriate for their setting.

PAMPHLET FOR STUDENTS

So You Are Going To Be In Group Counseling (Appendix E) is designed to indicate to potential group members and their parents what might occur in group and the purposes of groups. The pamphlet could be used in a group guidance situation where the notion of group counseling is being presented to a class by a counselor.

OPEN LETTER

For adult members the "Letter to a Fellow Group Member" (Appendix F) may be duplicated and given to members before or at the beginning of a group. The "Open Letter" was written by the authors of this text to articulate common concerns adults tend to have regarding groups. The first two paragraphs bring these concerns into focus. The third paragraph identifies some possible goals for individual members. The fourth and fifth paragraphs specify a member's responsibility. The next paragraph addresses communication in groups, while the final paragraph deals with helpful and unhelpful behaviors in groups. A leader may want to modify the "Open Letter" to suit the level of sophistication of his members. Readers have permission to reproduce "as is" or to edit in any way which seems appropriate.

THE PRE-GROUP INTERVIEW

The importance of the pre-group interview cannot be over-emphasized. The professional skill the leader brings to this induction process may well determine the initial success of the group. The counselor must devote as much time and energy to the group induction session as he would to any individual counseling session. Each prospective group member should explore in depth, in the privacy of the counseling office, his anticipations of group membership, his fantasies of what he imagines group might be like, what he expects to happen, how he expects to feel, will he like the experience, and does he fear it? Berne (1966) calls this fantasy of group life the

101

"group imago" and points out that this is private and unique for each member. Berne (ibid., p. 153) also claims that a member's "group imago" is the most decisive structural aspect for the outcome of an individual's therapy." The leader who explores each potential group member's fantasy concerning group membership will gain important idiosyncratic information about each member which will be useful in specifying objectives.

If the group counseling format calls for co-counselors, either of the counselors can conduct the pre-group interviews or each can conduct a portion of them. It is not necessary or desirable that both co-counselors interview an individual member.

During the pre-group interview the leader will make clear to potential members that there are no group goals *per se;* rather, there are for each individual member goals and objectives which it is hoped he will achieve through the group process. It is during this session that the leader and potential member jointly suggest and write down these specific objectives. In developing objectives, the counselee will begin to explore his self-perception, his values, his style of life, and his responsibility as a group member.

The setting of objectives is primary in that it provides direction and purpose for members and will provide outcome bench marks for group leaders. The following examples are for illustrative purposes only, to suggest how one counselor converted general goal statements to individual objectives.

Counselor: "Yes, Joe, to be in group counseling, we need to decide what you might want to get out of it."
(Note: The counselor does *not* ask Joe why he want to join a group!!!)

Joe: "Well, I am having trouble making friends. I never seem to have anyone to do things with. . . ."

Counselor: "Friends are something most people want. Let's consider what objectives we might decide on for you. Let's say perhaps you might make at least one friend from the members of the group. That seems reasonable to me."

Joe: "Yeah, I think that would be easy."

Counselor: "Then maybe we could hope that you might watch members in the group and figure out three ways others make friends . . . Does that seem possible?"

———

Mary: "Gosh, Mr. Johnson, I know I'm smart enough to get good grades but I just can't study or do my home-work."

Counselor: "Mary, I think the group might help you in this area. Let's think about some objectives you might realize out of group."

—"You might identify with different causes that keep you from doing your expected school assign-ments."

—"You might identify and try three techniques that will help you in organizing your priorities."

———

Peter: "Nobody trusts me and it makes me mad. My dad tells me to do something, then checks on me. I can't have the car when I really need it. They don't want me to have any fun."

Counselor: "I am experiencing a lot of anger in you. It's almost like no one listens to you or no one will let you grow up."

Peter: "I'm mad all right. I don't care about anything any-more."

Counselor: "Peter, the group might be able to help you. I think they will be able to give you feedback on what they feel and see. Let's set some outcomes that might help you in understanding yourself."

THE POST-GROUP INTERVIEW

After the final session, each participant should again be seen pri-vately; at this time he and the group leader can measure and discuss progress toward the objectives identified during the pre-group interview. A member may find that he achieved objectives which had not been anticipated either by the member or by the leaders. Some or all of the initial objectives may not have been realized. The main purpose of the post-group interview is to help a participant pull together his assessment of the group experience and to tie up any loose ends either the leader or members feel necessary. The purpose is *not* for leader or member to commiserate with one another regarding objectives not realized.

BIBLIOGRAPHY

Berne, Eric. *Principles of Group Treatment.* New York: Grove Press, 1966.

CHAPTER 7

CATALYSTS TO INTERACTION: A COLLECTION OF VERBAL CONFRONTATION TECHNIQUES

- Mild Confrontation
- Moderate Confrontation
- Intense Confrontation
- Bibliography

To the Group Leader:

These confrontation techniques are only as good as you are. Use them in wisdom.

CHAPTER 7

CATALYSTS TO INTERACTION: A COLLECTION OF VERBAL CONFRONTATION TECHNIQUES

The four functions of group leadership are observable to some degree in all interaction groups, although the theoretical constructs from which a leader works may vary. All group leaders perform some type of traffic-directing; all group leaders model in some way; all group leaders facilitate; all use some catalyst to interaction. In other models this catalyst may be silence or questioning or a suggested topic. In the Extensional model leaders move to confrontation quickly by using interaction stimulators to perform their leadership function of catalyst. To do this they may, at times, use interaction stimulators at mild, moderate, or intense levels. The "games" collected here are directed toward the catalytic function of group leadership. Leaders will need to use these techniques with skill and sensitivity. All require that the leaders "listen" with their eyes and ears at multi-levels, drawing on their extensive knowledge of the psychology of human behavior. The exercises are a *means* to an end, not an end in themselves, and should be used sparingly. It is recognized that these techniques represent a "cookbook" approach, but they are useful if used skillfully and discriminately. In the final analysis, the techniques are only as good as the skills of the leaders.

MILD CONFRONTATION

It is very likely that moving too far ahead of group members on the part of the group leader will inhibit rather than facilitate movement toward confrontation. Thus, it is wise to proceed with caution; the following suggestions represent only mild degrees of confrontation:

Birth Order. A very simple but usually productive device to encourage group members to look at themselves is to ask the group to subdivide into small groups according to whether the member was first born, last born, or middle born. Each group discusses problems which occurred in their lives as a result of their sibling position; then the entire group reassembles to share points of view. This technique will focus attention of present perceptions of group members as they talk about a productive topic of group content—individual members.

Territoriality. Asking a group which has been in session a time or two to change seats after the group has started will bring up the import of territoriality. Did group members tend to arrange themselves in the same seating order each time? How did they feel when they saw someone else sitting in their "territory"? Who sat next to whom on the rearrangement? What is each member's psychological territory? Another illustration of territoriality is made by asking group members to whisper in each other's ear and then to talk nose-to-nose. Acceptable social distances can be discussed before focusing on how close group members could comfortably sit next to other specific group members. The discussion of variations in distances leads to confrontations between group members.

Interaction Diagram. A simple sociometric device of asking group members to diagram with arrows the interactions of a given period of group discussion calls attention to cross-currents within the group. To whom is most interaction directed? Have the directions of output changed as the group has been developing? What is the effect of physical location, i.e., note ease of communicating across the circle as opposed to communicating with those not in direct eye contact.

First Memories. The recalling of first memories by group members may elicit mild confrontation. Members share with the group their very first memories in which there was an element of conflict. What was significant about that particular memory? Do group members perceive similarities in current behavior patterns which might create conflict?

Free Association. Free association can stimulate confrontation. The usual procedure is for the group leader to present a stimulus word which may or may not be "loaded" and ask group members to respond without thought around the circle. (Split-second censoring should be noted and perhaps called to the group's attention by the leader.) This technique tends to bring out affective content and is useful as a warmup process. "Going-round" is seldom completed more than a time or two before the group is dealing with significant materials.

"Druthers . . ." Begin the go-round with the sentence stem: "If I had my druthers I would be right now. . . ." This fantasy may help members explore their value systems, their action choices, and their self-acceptance.

Symbolic Substitution. Asking each member to fantasize what animal, or bird, or building, or geometric figure, or plant, or color, etc., he would like to be can be productive as members crystallize their perceptions of who they are. In using this "game" it is important that each member is asked to select a symbolic substitution for himself; members should not be permitted to label other members as an animal, etc. This is destructive and can lead to caricature.

New Names. Asking each member to select a new name for himself which is to be used in that group session and then allowing the group to react to that name may be a helpful way of exploring a sense of self which is deeply identified with names. Again, a member selects his own name; others do not choose for him.

Best Possible Way of Life. Asking members to describe their best possible way of life and then, perhaps, their worst possible way of life may assist members to identify where they are now on this continuum.

Stereotyping. Exploring stereotyping can lead to mild confrontation. One way this might be encouraged is by asking the group to respond to the group leader's third-person comment about a group member, such as, "Mary (a group member) sure thinks she is pretty good," and ask the group to share their immediate impressions concerning Mary. Then restate the comment, "Mary seems delightfully sure of herself." Again, the group can react. Mary can respond with *her* feelings, perhaps "going round" giving feedback to group members individually concerning her reactions to their comments.

Taking a Trip. Ask the group to imagine that each member is going on a trip and can take two people along from the group. Who would each member select? What is the reaction of those selected?

Presentation of Self: Clothing. The leader begins by suggesting that members make a statement about themselves in the clothing they select. From an almost infinite variety we selected (or someone did our selecting, which is significant) a wardrobe; then from the variety in our wardrobe, we selected the particular clothes we are wearing right now. Each of us is making some statement in this presentation of self through his clothing and it might be productive for each member to suggest what it is *he* sees himself transmitting by his clothes today.

The leader should begin by suggesting his ideas concerning his own clothes, such as seeing himself as conservative through his vest and grey suit, but a little rebellious by his choice of tie, etc., etc. As members explore their presentations of self, the leader should generalize to a characteristic way of behaving, to a life style.

Human Potential (Otto, 1970). The last procedure to be presented under mild confrontation techniques is a methodology rather than a technique, and an entire group counseling format could be built around these principles. The *Human Potential Seminar* is based on the assumption that something is *right* with the group member rather than, as is perhaps more usual, that something is *wrong* with him. The first step toward confrontation consists of "Strength Bombardment" in which one member volunteers to tell what his personal strengths are, after which the group responds by telling what strengths they see in him. The member then asks, "What do you see that is preventing me from using my strengths?" and again the group responds. The fourth step in the "Strength Bombardment" consists of group members constructing a group fantasy in which they imagine what the "target" person can be doing in five years or more if he uses his strengths optimally. As a final step the member is asked to relate to the group how he felt in undergoing this experience.

The second portion of the *Human Potential Seminar* consists of "Success Bombardment" in which a member begins by telling the group about the most successful experiences in his entire life and then follows up by telling about three fairly recent experiences which were unsuccessful. The group analyzes the unsuccesses in light of the success or achievement pattern revealed in the "Strength Bombardment" in order to make the member more aware of his own success pattern, to indicate whether failures represent non-application of his

110

success pattern, and to suggest areas where he has not tapped his potential.

The third section of the *Human Potential Seminar* is focused on action and consists of goal-setting experiences. At the close of each session members in the group set *individual* goals which are to be accomplished before the next meeting. The goals must be: (1) capable of being put into words, (2) believable, (3) measurable, (4) something the members really want to do, and (5) presented with no alternatives. The purpose of this procedure is to help members become aware that they can control their own lives to a far greater degree than they probably do at the present time. It also helps members become aware of their own value systems and increase self-motivation. The *Human Potential Seminar* is a small group educational experience which makes use of the confrontation level of interaction in a planned sequence.

MODERATE CONFRONTATION

The following interaction techniques involve a higher degree of risk than do the preceding procedures. The "games" delineated in the following section require fairly intensive involvement and move to a confrontive level rather quickly.

Slides. A series of slides may be presented which represent highly charged situations. Members are asked to respond with their feelings toward the scenes with the goal of enabling them to get in touch with their feelings as they occur and to be aware of the particular zone of the body where they occur. The slides selected should have an emotional overlay and should represent a wide range of emotions. It is essential that the slides be in color.

The group leader should project the slides on the screen, at first leaving the picture showing for a minute, then immediately discussing with the group their reactions to that slide. Gradually, the time spans the stimuli are given should be decreased and discussion need not take place after each picture. The leader should use his own reactions to the pictures, being careful not to imply that his are the correct ones. As the experience develops the leader may choose to react to the members as *they* react, thus making the interaction more and more personal and "here and now."

Pictures of Members. Another way of using slides is for the leader using a hand camera to make pictures of each member at one meeting. At the next meeting each member and the leader will have his image projected onto the screen and the group will interact. A word of caution: with the use of slides of members care must be taken that members do not experience themselves as objects or that the interaction becomes a "critique" session.

Magic Shop. Another moderate confrontation procedure is termed "Magic Shop" and consists of an approach whereby the group is asked to imagine that they can shop at a magic place in which only intangibles are in stock. Any intangible, such as honesty, love, great intelligence, etc., may be purchased, but the price is something which the individual already owns, such as good health, joy of living, intelligence, etc. The Magic Shop is an excellent device to confront group members with their value systems and the commitment each may have to any given set of values.

A possible variation is to suggest that members may obtain anything from the Magic Shop but need not return anything, or may give up something they wish to discard.

Role-Playing. A common confrontation technique, but one which is too little used in group counseling, is role-playing. An alert leader can easily find appropriate situations arising out of content which group members provide wherein role-playing can be useful. It is important to use the technique of role reversal and it is important to provide sufficient time in the group session to explore thoroughly the implications of the role play. The insights gained through skillful use of this confrontation technique usually are most satisfactory.

Identifying Emotions. Two simple confrontation procedures aimed at the conative level of awareness involve emotions. The first asks group members to list quickly all the emotions they can. Then lists are compared and differing lengths and contents are discussed relative to the affect which each group member transmits. An additional exercise involves asking group members to communicate to the group the emotion in awareness at a given time. Then the member is asked to bring up from the "back" of his mind the next emotion, continually free associating, discarding one emotion as another is brought

112

into awareness. The purpose of the group leader is to help group members become aware of their on-going feelings, tap their stream of consciousness, tune inward on visceral reactions, and gain in skill of verbalizing these feelings.

Drifting. Another possible confrontation-encouraging procedure is called "drifting." In this exercise the group leader asks the group to drift aimlessly about the room without talking. No further instruction is given, but the group can be seen to divide into subgroups— who with whom?—and some members will return to their seats more quickly than others. The ensuing discussion brings focus on group members' tendencies toward conformity, their degree of independence, their tolerance for ambiguity, their compulsivity of goals, their self-consciousness in the face of an unstructured field, and their need for territoriality.

Symbolic Objects. The leader begins the group by asking each member to select some thing or things concrete from the environment which symbolizes himself. The area from which to select can be as extensive as time and area allow.

When members return to the group, each presents his object and describes how his object symbolizes him. The leader should make a selection and begin the interaction by his presentation. For example, he might have chosen keys for his object and then might describe these keys as representing himself searching for answers, always looking for ways to open doors to truth, or looking for ways to unlock relationships with people, *etc.*

Micro-lab. The micro-lab is one of the most useful exercises to encourage confrontation and can be used to initiate a series of group encounters.

Directions for the micro-lab are to be given as follows: Each group is divided into two sub-groups for the purpose of this exercise. Sub-group composition remains the same for the duration of the exercise. Sub-groups are labeled "A" and "B." To begin the exercise group A meets for seven minutes. While group A is meeting in a small circle, group B sits outside that circle observing the members of group A. Each member of group A has a "feedback partner" in group B— this is determined by the schedule in Figure 7-1 below.

After group A has met for seven minutes it breaks for a four-minute

FIGURE 7-1
SCHEDULE FOR MICRO-LAB

GROUP	9 MEMBERS	8 MEMBERS	7 MEMBERS	6 MEMBERS	ROUND
A	1 2 3 4 x	1 2 3 4	1 2 3 x	1 2 3	
B	5 6 7 8 9	5 6 7 8	4 5 6 7	4 5 6	I
A	1 2 3 4 x	1 2 3 4	1 2 3 x	1 2 3	
B	9 5 6 7 8	8 5 6 7	7 4 5 6	6 4 5	II
A	1 2 3 4 x	1 2 3 4	1 2 3 x	1 2 3	
B	8 9 5 6 7	7 8 5 6	6 7 4 5	5 6 4	III
A	1 2 3 4 x	1 2 3 4	1 2 3 x	1 2 3	
B	7 8 9 5 6	6 7 8 5	5 6 7 4	4 5 6	VI
A	1 2 3 4 x	1 2 3 4	1 2 3 x	1 2 3	
B	6 7 8 9 5	5 6 7 8	4 5 6 7	6 4 5	V

(ROUNDS VI THROUGH X SAME AS I THROUGH V)

feedback session during which each individual in group A will receive feedback on his seven minutes of behavior from his partner in group B. When the feedback session is concluded, group B meets in the small circle which group A observes. When seven minutes of activity is terminated the four-minute feedback session again occurs, with individuals in group A giving feedback to the same individuals in group B who had initially given them feedback. At this point partners shall be changed according to the schedule above. Always change partners at the point where both have given each other feedback. After partners have changed, the process is continued as indicated above. Before the first meeting a timekeeper is selected in each subgroup. The sub-group on the outside times the inside group for the seven- and four-minute periods.

Significant Experiences. A final moderate confrontation exercise involves a "going round." Each group member is asked to make a specified number of statements about himself which should be personal. The group then reacts. A variation of this procedure involves the use of a timer. The leader sets the timer for a selected amount of

114

time—perhaps three minutes—and each group member uses the time to tell about himself. Both this procedure and the short statement procedure described above should be initiated by the leader who sets the stage by being the first to tell about himself.

INTENSE CONFRONTATION

The final group of interaction techniques encourages involvement on a very deep personal basis. These procedures should not be used too early in a group's life or strong resistance to the group process may be created.

Mirror Image. The first procedure is called "mirror image." A group member is asked to look at himself in a mirror and describe what he sees as honestly as he can. Group members then give feedback, agreeing or disagreeing.

Behind the Back. The behind-the-back technique must be used particularly carefully, but it focuses a group at the confrontation level. In this exercise a group member who is "target" is asked to turn his chair around and face away from the group. Group members then discuss him as if he were not present. After the discussion the member who is the behind-the back focus turns around and reacts to the previous comments. During both phases of this exercise it is vital that the group leader be active in helping members interact.

First Impressions. Members are asked to recall and report uncensored their first impressions of others in the group. This must be on a very personal level to be productive.

Authority Figure "Hangups." The group leader might also tap members' insights into their reactions to authority figures by asking the group to put down on a piece of paper as many or as few dots as each member wishes, then to try to connect these dots with a line which does not cross itself. As the group does this, the group leader expresses disapproval—shaking his head and looking rather disgusted. He then announces that he will give the group one more trial, at which time he transmits no approval or disapproval but merely sits indifferently. The discussion can focus on the group members' reactions to an authority figure's disapproval concerning a task which obviously can be accomplished and the feelings this inappropriate disapproval engendered within them. Where is their focus of evaluation? Another area for discussion might be the various life styles demonstrated by group members as they approach this task—were they serious, committed, uninvolved? Did members put down many dots or few? How long did each continue under disapproval? Did the disapproval create group unity? Did behavior during the second opportunity differ from the first? Did the group leader's attitude change behavior? How do group members respond to and handle authority figures?

Autobiographies. The capsule autobiography can be used to effect confrontation. Each group member is asked to write five or so sentences concerning his life history. These are read by the leader and discussed anonymously. Is there a life theme (a script)? Group members will gain understanding of the life space of other group members and may gain insight into their own life space. Focus may also dwell on future plans. Confrontation will be gained in this exercise if the group leader is familiar with projective theory.

Group Sociogram. Asking the group to draw a sociogram of the group after it has been in session at least once can hasten confrontation as members examine interpersonal relations within the group and speculate on causes. Who are isolates? Who are stars? After a period of sessions will or did the sociograms change?

Rejection. An example in deliberate rejection can be used to dwell on hostile feelings. Group members are asked to totally ignore one member who attempts to integrate with the group either physically and/or verbally. The feelings engendered in all group members are worth exploring at a confrontation level.

Masks. Interaction may be stimulated if the leader asks each member to imagine that he removes the mask he wears. The group participants then describe how they see themselves with their masks removed.

Twenty-four Hours to Live. The leader fantasizes that the group has discovered that each member has only twenty-four hours to live.

In turn, the participants describe how they would spend the time.

Three Adjectives. In a "go-round" procedure each member is asked to describe himself with three adjectives. The group interacts as each member makes his suggestions.

What Would You Like to Be Remembered For?: Suggesting that members explore the memories of themselves they would like to stand on as their "signatures of essence" may help identify for participants their value structures and the ways in which they are translating those values into action. For example, one member might want to be remembered for the friends he made, or that he loved someone very deeply, or he might not want to be remembered at all —whatever statements are made can be explored productively.

Id Color and Shape: Asking psychologically sophisticated groups to explore their fantasies concerning their ids as to color and shape can be most productive. The implications for core of personality and life styles are profound.

As a Group Member . . . Toward the end of the group sessions it is often helpful to ask members to complete the sentence "As A Group Member I . . ." This triggers exploration of the meaning of the experience for each participant, the commitment he has to the group, and perhaps what he wants or has obtained from the group experience.

Freezing: When group content seems to be drifting off to the there and then, it is sometimes helpful to ask members to "freeze" and to elicit feedback from group members concerning their feelings.

Legitimizing: A useful go-around is to ask each member to specify the characteristic he has which he feels needs legitimizing. For example, a member might suggest that he feels his need to manipulate, or his sexuality, or his inability to sustain friendships, may need legitimizing; that is, he feels that they are a part of him that is not accepted by others. Group members can provide feedback concerning their reactions to the member's quest. Leaders will need to be alert at this point that members do not begin "Super-mothering" in an effort to legitimize. The former involves a denial of a member's reality; the latter involves complete acceptance and recognition of that member's reality.

Blank Space: Provide each member with a blank sheet of paper and ask him to project his life space onto that paper. Allow several minutes of silence while this occurs. Then go around and ask each member to describe whatever elements of his paper he wishes to, then as each member completes his description, ask for feedback to that member before moving on to the next person. Leaders facilitate the understanding of life styles, values, and so forth by their verbal reactions, performing their modeling function and their facilitating function.

A refinement of this procedure is to ask that each member physically do something with his sheet of paper at the end of his presentation. A member might then throw it on the floor, might sit on it, might hold it close to his body, might hold it out to others. Whatever he does provides profound material for exploration and legitimizing.

Choosing a Family. Members select a "family" from group members—a mother, father, younger sibling, older sibling, spouse, son, and daughter. For the purposes of this exercise the sex of group members is ignored. The group then discusses the selections. The degree of frankness with which the procedure is carried out, of course, depends on the group leader. Throughout all the exercises it will be his attitude, skill, and activity which insure success.

Personal Constructs. Three students who are interested in learning the impression the group has of them volunteer to be "targets." The group then suggests ways in which any two of the three volunteers are alike or different from the third. This exercise dwells on the "here and now" of the group process and group members—the level at which behavioral change is most likely to take place.

Twin Selector. A procedure somewhat similar to the preceding exercise involves asking each member to select three members of the group who resemble him most. He then is to state the reasons for his selections and the group gives feedback.

New Ways of Behaving. For a specified time group members are asked to try out a way of behaving which they see as desirable, but which they have not previously seen themselves as doing. Five minutes may be sufficient for the exercise if the group is not too large. At the end of the designated time members are asked to report to the group what "new" behaviors they observed in others, to react to their own "new" behavior, and to report feelings involved.

Psychodrama and Sociodrama. Reporting the procedures particular to psychodrama and sociodrama is beyond the scope of this book, but the use of this method seems to hold promise for group counseling. Some adaptation may be needed for the school setting.

The preceding techniques may be useful as devices to encourage a group to focus on the "here and now," "I and Thou," but the main instrument of movement toward confrontation is the group leader himself. If he is willing to risk himself in encounter, the group is likely to follow. If he is not, the group probably will remain at a safe, nonproductive, topic-centered level.

BIBLIOGRAPHY

Otto, Herbert A. *Group Methods to Actualize Human Potential.* Beverly Hills: The Holistic Press, 1970.

CHAPTER 8

CATALYSTS TO INTERACTION: A COLLECTION OF NONVERBAL CONFRONTATION TECHNIQUES

- Body Language
    - Hands and Feet
    - The Face
    - Body Posture
- Territoriality
- Nonverbal Exercises
    - Body Language Exercises
    - Territoriality Exercises
- Summary
- Bibliography

To the Group Leader:

Nonverbal language speaks as loudly to the leader as does verbal language. The purpose of this chapter is to sensitize you to these messages and to enable you to sensitize your group members to them.

CHAPTER 8

CATALYSTS TO INTERACTION: A COLLECTION OF NONVERBAL CONFRONTATION TECHNIQUES

The thumb tucked tightly inside a fist, a flexing jaw muscle, arms folded tightly across a chest, the drumming of an index finger, the selection of a floor cushion as a seat—all represent important messages to group leaders. While they may not respond verbally to these silent signals the facilitating function of leaders requires that they observe and draw tentative meanings from them. When verbal and nonverbal cues seem incongruent, when the tone of voice says one thing while the words say another, when lips are smiling but hands are clenched, the leader's vigilance system is on full force. The language of nonverbal communications in group is rich with silent signals which can be received by a leader's sensitive antennas. The leader "hears" as many of these signals as possible; he responds selectively.

There is some research which indicates that specific nonverbal behaviors do have specific psychological meaning (Mahl, 1968; Mehrabian, 1968; Ekman and Friesen, 1968; Beier, 1966). For the present such evidence must be viewed as tentative; however, Mahl's 1968 study of gestures and body movements seems most relevant. He suggests that certain specific acts seem to be expressing the same kinds of feelings in all his subjects. For example, making a fist, rubbing one's nose, shrugging shoulders, interest in fingernails, and interest in teeth generally indicate hostility. Self-scratching is usually seen as turning hostility around on self. A person who sits rigidly erect with hands folded in his lap is seen as exerting rigid controls over hostile and aggressive impulses. The frequency of rapid foot movements and general postural shifts provide a good estimate of overall anxiety.

Mehrabian (1968) reported that posture may indicate both liking and status. The more a person leans toward the person he is speaking to, the more positively he feels about him. Direct eye contact may also be an indication of positive regard, while habitual avoidance of eye contact may be an expression of dislike or fear.

The above findings must be viewed as tentative, for other writers indicate that messages sent nonverbally do not have universal meanings (Hall, 1959). Group leaders, however, need not be tentative about increasing their awareness of nonverbal group behavior, however tentative their interpretation of the meanings of the silent signals. They should be alert to changes of posture, relaxation of muscles, and tensing of muscles. They can note changes in rates of speech, direction of gaze, length of messages and silences, change in facial expressions, and members' postures. Below you will find described some of the nonverbal behaviors which seem important to us; you will no doubt want to lengthen the list.

But first, an important issue should be addressed: What can group leaders do once they have noted a specific nonverbal behavioral response in a group member? There are at least two alternatives. One alternative is for them to offer their feelings concerning the behavior in question. For example, if a member is answering "yes" verbally in response to a question, but is at the same time shaking his head "no," the leader may feel confused by this contradictory set of responses and let the member know it. It must be kept in mind that a perception of nonverbal behavior given by the leader or any group member is the private feeling of the speaker holding the view, and the person producing the behavior may choose to accept or reject such views as he pleases.

The second possibility will be the one most frequently used by the leaders. They simply note the behavior silently, storing it away as tentative information concerning the group member, using this added knowledge to make better judgments as they proceed with the group process.

Frequently group members will not be aware of the nonverbal messages they are sending, and the question arises of whether the leaders are indulging in psychological voyeurism when they observe and try to understand meanings behind their observations. Perhaps the most honest way to handle this dilemma is for the leaders to comment in their introductory remarks that they will be attempting to communicate at all levels throughout the group process, and this includes nonverbal cues. At this point, the leaders might ask group members to react to their nonverbal behaviors and try to articulate their responses to these cues.

When a leader first chooses to react verbally to a nonverbal cue, members become self-conscious and uncomfortable, and this, too, should be discussed openly. Once members understand that non-verbal language is only an extension of verbal language, they can come to terms with the fact that they are transmitting messages constantly, consciously or unconsciously, and these messages are being received constantly, consciously or unconsciously.

The following comments describe silent signals sent through a person's nonverbal body language and silent signals sent in relation to others. Under "Body Language" messages transmitted through posture, face, and hands and feet, are described while nonverbal communications sent in relation to others have been subsumed under "Territoriality." Focus is on increasing the observational skills of group leaders so as to enhance their facilitating function.

The various nonverbal confrontation techniques which follow might be used to help group members become more sensitive to their own and others' silent signals. The leader will need to exercise judgment as he introduces these non-verbal catalysts into the group process. Obviously he should have a specific purpose in mind for selecting any given exercise. At times the purpose may suggest that the entire group be involved, while at other times an exercise should only be used to clarify a relationship between two members.

The general area of the *Hill Interaction Matrix* which seems to the writers to be tapped by a particular exercise is identified. Subsequent verbal interaction may or may not fall into the same cells as targeted by the nonverbal exercise.

A word of caution to the leaders: the translation of silent signals is as much an art as a science; thus it is important to remember that the following suggestions for interpretation must invariably be weighed against the contents of the conative universe of the person reacting to the message.

BODY LANGUAGE

Body Language may be "spoken" by the body as a whole or by

various parts of the body. Several messages may be sent simultaneously, and at times these messages may contradict each other. A signal sent by one person may mean something entirely different when sent by another. Thus the meaning which might be attached to a nonverbal cue depends on the sender, on the situation, and on the receiver. Any interpretations of common nonverbal cues can only be on the basis of a very, very tentative hypothesis which a group leader might give to silent signals sent by group members through their body language. This language will be "translated" from three areas: hands and feet, face, and posture.

Hands and Feet

The thumb tightly enclosed within the fist may suggest to group leaders to proceed with caution, while a member who has both thumbs within his fists sends an even stronger "red flag" message. Hands palms up possibly transmits a non-defensive stance suggesting a willingness to receive messages. Hands obscuring the mouth may indicate a desire to communicate coupled with some hesitancy in doing so. Hands folded with fingers interlaced, palms loose and out, might suggest some willingness to interact but with reservations, while the same hand position with fingers tightly folded and the mounts of the thumbs pressed firmly together possibly indicates a higher degree of defensiveness. A twirling of a ring or the fingering of jewelry may be symptomatic of inner tensions. Cracking of knuckles suggests aggression as well as tension and rigidity. All of these observations can only form the basis for *possible* cues to inner behaviors, but for the group leaders who have a responsibility to be alert to all cues, verbal and nonverbal, hands are a rich source of data.

Twisting hands, shaking hands, wet hands, cold hands, clenched hands, open hands, outward reaching hands, inward pointing hands, the shaken finger, the raised fist, index fingers across pursed lips—all may contain messages of importance to the group leader. Feet also send messages; these messages may be more easily missed than the messages sent by the hands. Group leaders should constantly scan the group for feet which are tapping or moving in a rhythmic manner. The message sent is most certainly one of inner tension. The tension may mean that the member is attending to the group very intently, or it may mean that the member would like to escape from the current

126

interchange. Leaders cannot be sure of the exact meaning of any silent signal, but they can be sure that the signal *has* a meaning.

The crossing of feet may mean a member is closing off open communication, warding off threats, rejecting the group as a whole, rejecting a particular member of the group, or any number of other possible interpretations. Feet stretched out into a group are probably sending a different message from feet tucked up under a body or feet slid back under a chair. The removal of shoes from feet usually signals relaxation, while feet slipping in and out of shoes may indicate ambivalence concerning what is happening in the group. Pant creases tightening at the knees probably indicates an increase in muscle tension through legs and feet. The tracing of a figure eight or a circle with a toe may indicate involvement in the group on the part of the member who is "talking" this signal. Two female feet placed flat on the floor close together suggests a sexual attitude different from that expressed by other available foot postures. Two male feet pressed firmly to the floor with two hands pressing downward on the knees certainly sends a message of aggression. The way group members arrange one leg in relation to the other usually sends messages. Shifts in these body stances also send messages. Obviously the group leader cannot take in all nonverbal cues, and he most certainly cannot read these cues accurately all the time, but with practice and attention a surprising number can be processed.

The Face

Mehrabian (ibid.) showed that facial expression transmits over 55 percent of the meaning of a message. Group leaders can improve their effectiveness by learning to process the complex yet fleeting messages that the face expresses. These messages are sent by group members whether they are speaking, listening, or withdrawn. Expressions range from those connoting boredom and daydreaming to expressions indicating excitement and growth.

Of all facial features the eyes probably send the most accurate messages. Although the volume of messages from this area of the face is beyond human handling, group leaders will process what they can as accurately as possible. Closed eyes may indicate a temporary flight—into self or away from the field. The absence of eye contact may signal a retreat to an "I-It" relationship—certainly the nonverbal message concerns some loss of "I-Thou" communication.

The member who appears to be unwilling to sustain eye contact may prefer to relate to people as objects and probably tends to intellectualize as a characteristic defense mechanism. Such a person often can be observed shifting from a momentary eye-to-eye connection with another group member to "seeing" into space behind the addressed member, where he disconnects from others and "looks at" an idea or into himself. By this time he is essentially talking to himself and has phased out any relationship with another. The eye contact circuit breaks and the human connection seems to lose power. On the other hand, the member who constantly looks to the group leader probably is seeking approval and may need to explore dependency patterns. The member who glares with widened eyes is hard to misunderstand. The eyes hidden by dark glasses send a message. Eyes drifting out of the group speak rather loudly. Eyes glancing covertly at watches suggest a meaning which is almost unmistakable. Rapid eye movements may suggest a search for an exit. Rapid eyeblinking sometimes indicates intense disagreement or strong emotional reactions.

Nonverbal expression related to the mouth and voice offers another rich set of behavioral patterns to the attentive eyes and ears of group leaders. The smile which is not in harmony with a verbal message is usually quite apparent, as is the self-abnegating laugh, the nervous giggle, or the clearing of the throat. Group members' voices can either lack impact—hollow, droning, meek, submissive, tentative —or be rich, mellow, and commanding. A voice can be a little boy's or a little girl's voice, or the voice of mama or daddy. Each person's voice sends a usually unconscious message about the sender. A group leader can bring part of the quality of a member's voice to his awareness through the use of listening to tapes of group sessions.

Nonverbal messages cannot be read with certainty. To suggest that such is the case is irresponsible, but to ignore them is equally irresponsible. Group leaders must attempt to observe as many of these signals as possible, but do not necessarily respond verbally. The majority of silent signals will be processed silently by the leaders until they feel that a verbal recognition will be helpful.

Body Posture

Facial cues and hand and foot cues are two important sources of nonverbal data. Another source is general body posture. A torso leaning into a group; an upright rigidly-held torso; a slumped, relaxed torso—all send quite different messages. Deep sighs, rapid breathing, a rising flush, the head in hands, chewing on nails, changes of head and neck postures, changes in overall body postures, the authoritative shaking of a finger or a pencil, doodling, the subtle pushing back of chairs, removing of coats, loosening of ties, clicking of nails, chewing on glasses, taking glasses on and off are silent signals which are constantly being sent throughout a group when members are settled into session.

Eric Berne's (1961) analysis of body posture from the theoretical framework of transactional analysis contains material which the group leader should find helpful. Berne suggests that body stance communicates information concerning which of the three (parent, child, or adult) ego states is in control at any given time. For example, an index finger shaking at the group suggests that the member is "coming on" in a parent ego state, while a slumped shoulder posture may indicate a child ego state. Group leaders who familiarize themselves with Berne's work will find body posture a rich source of data concerning members' inner worlds.

Posture messages are sent in many ways. For example, a drastic change in mode of dress may indicate a change of attitude toward the group on the part of an individual member, and also may indicate a change of general group climate. Alert leaders will observe which members arrive together and which members leave together. Do individual members exhibit separation anxieties when the group session ends? These anxieties are almost always sent nonverbally, and responsible leaders are sensitive to them.

TERRITORIALITY

An area of nonverbal behavior closely related to the types of behaviors mentioned above is that of territoriality, i.e., what invisible lines does a person draw around himself which define his life space? Where do his boundaries end and how much neutral territory does he attempt to establish between himself and another? How easy is it

129

for a group member to "invade" the territory of another? How do various members handle such invasions of their territory? The amount of life space a group member unconsciously declares as his territory is observable through noting whether a member moves his chair into the circle or shifts it closer to another or positions himself so as to have maximum space between his chair or body and others in the group. In general, it is likely that the person who maintains an unusually wide physical distance between his life space and that of another will also find it more comfortable to maintain the same psychological distance, and, in all probability, exerts a great deal of psychic energy maintaining a rigid defense system.

As leaders become sensitized to territoriality signals they might note the choice of a corner by a group member as making a different statement from that made by the choice of sitting on the floor at the foot of the leader. They might note how sub-groups arrange themselves in relation to various ages within the group. Do members arrange themselves in relation to various age groups? In relation to sexes? Who tends to bring the coffee? Who tends to see that cups are filled? Who arrives early? Late? Who tends to miss meetings? All of these nonverbal choices carry some meaning; the translation of these choices into meanings and the importance of the meanings must be left up to the sensitivity of the leader who is always aware of his own biases and limitations, which inevitably distort input and therefore make it imperative that all interpretations remain tentative.

It is important that leaders observe territoriality statements, however, as the data provide them with information concerning areas to explore and areas to avoid. A member who enters the group and scans the "territory" to locate competition or to locate support is more vigilant and therefore probably more defensive than is the member who enters the group and immediately makes some sort of nonverbal contact with all other members. The member who establishes his territory near the door may be perceiving the group quite differently than does a member who finds the corner more comfortable. It is the business of the leader to take in as many of these signals as he can, even though he awaits validation from other behaviors, both verbal and nonverbal.

NONVERBAL EXERCISES

Often a group member will complain that he can't feel trust, love, caring for another, aggressive feelings, or a sense of who he is. The member expresses a lack of feeling and indicates to the group leader and group members that he wants to experience these feelings. Often it will happen that the leader and members will have already noticed nonverbal behavior hinting at the presence of these supposedly non-existing feelings. For example, if the member claims he can't feel angry, yet is perpetually frowning, the leader may suggest that the member try exaggerating this frown and include with the exaggeration any other nonverbal (or verbal) behavior that tends to arise. The idea of amplifying or exaggerating an attitude or behavior is a potent source from which the individual can become aware of feelings which are his but for some reason or other remain below his present level of awareness.

A host of nonverbal techniques for helping people "get into their feelings" can be used by the skillful group leader. He will learn through experience when the time is ripe for a particular exercise that might help a member break through into a new compartment of his feeling self. A leader must be cautious in using these exercises lest they end up forcing the member to become defensive, and therefore less likely to experience his own feelings.

Group leaders who are working with students in an institutional or public school setting also must exercise caution in the use of these exercises. Physical contact probably is inappropriate and those non-verbal experiences which require such contact should be avoided. The suggestion as to the general area of the *Hill Interaction Matrix* (*HIM*) which seems tapped by a specific exercise may give direction to the group leaders as to which of these nonverbal catalysts to use with a particular group. Obviously the setting as well as the sophistication of the group must be taken into consideration.

The following exercises are presented in two areas—those which deal primarily with body language and those which deal primarily with territoriality.

Body Language Exercises

Eye Contact is a good exercise for testing sensitivity to nonverbal facial messages. A member in this exercise comes into contact with his feelings that are associated with being looked at by another and with looking at another. Group members pair into dyads and silently look into one another's eyes and face for thirty seconds. Over a period of several group meetings leaders may want to gradually increase the time interval to the point where members become comfortable with the process, and communicating with eye contact becomes routine group behavior. This exercise should encourage members to become more open with and sensitive to others.

(HIM Cell: This exercise seems to deal mainly with the Conventional-Relationship cell of the HIM.)

Deep Breathing. Deep breathing can be used to open a group session once a group has been taught the technique, which is quite different from the usual drawing air vigorously in and out of the nostrils. This "Yoga" approach to deep breathing involves a "tuning in" to one's inner world of proprioception and in particular to the expansion and contraction feelings of the ribcage accompanying breathing. Members can be directed to fill the lower part of their lungs with air first, then the middle part, and finally the upper part. In exhaling, the upper part, then the middle, and last the lower part of the lungs is emptied. The chest remains motionless and passive while the ribs expand during inhalation and contract during exhalation. Breathe in to the count of four, hold for two counts, and exhale to four counts. Ten or twelve deep breaths will be relaxing and will help members get in touch with the ribcage and lungs. (A more extensive description of the techniques of deep breathing can be found in Devi's book *Yoga for Americans* (1959).

(HIM Cell: The HIM cells touched by this simple exercise appear to be Personal-Conventional).

Body Relaxation. An exercise which can be used to follow the few minutes of deep breathing involves the leader asking members to sit up straight in their chairs and put both feet flat on the floor with closed eyes. (In an appropriate setting, this exercise can be done with the members lying flat on their backs on the floor.) Leader then "talks" quietly up the body, beginning with the feet, asking members to relax the muscles in their left foot, then their right foot. Next the leader moves to the left and right lower legs, knees, etc. This is done very slowly and members' eyes remain closed throughout the entire exercise. The period ends with a few minutes of silence. This procedure allows members to get in touch with their bodies, as well as to relax their muscle systems.

(HIM Cell: The HIM Conventional-Personal cell seems mainly drawn on here.)

Transmitting Emotions. In this exercise members are asked to transmit various emotions nonverbally. Leaders ask members to pair into dyads. They then hand one of the dyads a card on which is written an emotion—anger, trust, love, fear, hate, sympathy, or tenderness. Only one emotion is given at a time and each of the dyads can take turns or can work with different emotions. When the exercise is completed, the group discusses the experience: what part of the body was most effective in transmitting a particular emotion? how accurate was the receiver in guessing the emotion which was being transmitted? did the transmitter feel the emotion and if so where? how were hands used, eyes, mouth, sounds, body stance? A variation of this exercise involves describing one's feelings in this situation using gibberish or nonsense language.

One of the byproducts of this exercise is the highlighting of the necessity of verbal feedback in groups. The contradictory nonverbal and verbal messages which are sometimes sent should be explored. The need to validate with verbal communication is underscored by the difficulty members probably will experience in "reading" accurately the nonverbal emotions.

(HIM Cell: Relationship-Conventional seems the area of the Matrix tapped by this exercise.)

Masks. A follow-up of the above exercise can be done with masks. Leaders provide full-face plastic masks. These can be purchased in a variety store, especially around Halloween. Members are asked to go through the previous exercise, but with all facial expressions obscured; thus only the body is available to transmit the emotions. Members may become aware of gross body movements which they use in nonverbal communication, or they may realize that they use their bodies very little to communicate. Again, discussion *always* follows each exercise.

(HIM Cell: As in the previous exercise, "Masks" mainly interacts in the Relationship-Conventional mode.)

Nonverbal Encounter. In this exercise a member who has some-

133

thing to express toward another group member is asked to volunteer. He and his partner stand at opposite ends of the room and slowly approach each other before the entire group. The ensuing encounter is completely on a nonverbal level; masks can be used as a variation of the technique. When the pair has finished, each discusses his feelings and the whole group discusses what it has observed. In this way the participants become aware of messages which might otherwise escape their notice.

(HIM Cell: This exercise is very likely to center in the Relationship-Assertive area of the Matrix.)

Slides. A series of slides may be prepared and projected onto a screen. Members are asked to respond as quickly as possible with the primary emotion elicited by the slide and then asked to specify where in their body they felt the emotion. The leader interacts with the members as they respond to the slides, attempting to identify where in his body he is receiving members' communications as they interact. As a result of this experience, members may find an increased awareness of their body responses and also may enlarge their awareness of the wide range of human responses elicited by a similar stimuli. The content of the slides must be appropriate for the intended audience. For example, for an adult group a picture of a naked man and woman might be appropriate but would be eliminated for a student group in a school setting.

A variation of the slides for emotions might be to take pictures of workers in a number of occupations and project these onto the screen. Group members can explore their emotional reactions as well as their values in connection with vocational roles. This procedure would be appropriate for any grade level.

(HIM Cell: The Slides stimuli seem to tap the Personal-Conventional area of the HIM.)

Relay. The old parlor game of "gossip" can be adapted to a useful nonverbal communication exercise. The leader asks group members to close their eyes. He then whispers to a member an emotion which is to be transmitted to the next member, and so on around the circle. The member who is to transmit the message to the next member attempts to do so nonverbally, using any portion of his body he wishes. When the exercise begins only the two members involved in the immediate transmission are to have their eyes open, but as each one finishes, he can observe the remaining members' attempts to communicate nonverbally, and thus become more aware of body language signals. Each receiver is alerted by a touch which signals him to open his eyes and receive the nonverbal "message." At the end of the exercise, the last member verbalizes what he feels was transmitted to him and the group discusses the experience. Leaders may choose to use this exercise to emphasize the importance of verbal feedback to open communication.

(HIM Cell: This exercise seems to deal with Conventional-Relationship.)

Lifting. If circumstances are appropriate, the lifting and trust exercise can be used by leaders who want to explore trust in the group as a whole or in certain members. This exercise also tends to increase a member's feeling of belonging to the group. Members stand in a circle shoulder to shoulder facing inward, while one member stands in the center inside the circle with closed eyes. When the member in the middle feels relaxed the members of the circle pass the person in the center one to another for a brief time and then gently lift him up over their heads, moving him back and forth in a swaying motion. The exercise concludes with the group lowering the member to the floor very slowly and gently. The entire exercise is done in complete silence. Discussion begins when all who wish have gone through the experience, and may center around an individual member's difficulty in trusting.

(HIM Cell: This exercise seems to focus mainly on the Speculative-Relationship of the HIM.)

Trust. The experience of trust can also be explored by a nonverbal exercise which asks one member to fall backward into the arms of another without hesitation. The receiving member breaks the fall with his arms. Many members are unable to fall back without first checking that the other person or persons is there. Others cannot allow themselves to fall at all. (It is important that very small women do not attempt to catch very large men, but in general most people can catch one another without danger to either.) The subsequent discussion should be productive concerning the ability to trust, and general views of the trustworthiness of others. The general life styles of members in relation to their perceptions of others will emerge.

(HIM Cell: The Trust exercise explores mainly from the Personal and Relationship of the Conventional Cells.)

Nonverbal Go-Around. The opportunity for each group member and the leader to communicate nonverbally with all other group members provides a moving experience. The group leader asks all members to stand up and move into a comfortable close circle, facing inward, shoulders almost touching. Each member in turn steps into the inner perimeter of the circle and, facing outward, moves from one member to another, attempting to communicate nonverbally his feelings for each other member. The leader begins this exercise and thus sets the tone. The entire exercise is completed in silence. When all members and leaders have had an opportunity to interact with each other, the group takes their seats and discusses the experience. Most groups find this a deeply moving experience and the subsequent discussion will demonstrate an increased group solidarity and heightened sensitivity to each other.

(HIM Cell: The Relationship-Confrontive cell of the HIM will be the area tapped by the nonverbal exercise, although, of course, the subsequent discussion may dwell in any of the cells.)

Videotape Feedback. The use of videotape as a tool to facilitate group interaction is addressed more thoroughly elsewhere in this manual, but brief mention will be made here concerning the use of this tool as a technique to help group members become aware of both their body language and their territoriality signals. One member of the group or the co-leader can run the camera, which should be equipped with both a wide-angle and a closeup lens. A fairly brief segment of group interaction is taped. The cameraman attempts to focus mainly on nonverbal cues sent by a speaker and by the listeners. The tape is then played to the group either with or without sound and discussion can focus on nonverbal messages being transmitted throughout the group.

(HIM Cell: The videotape experience will tap Personal-Confrontive primarily, although the subsequent discussion may range into all cells of the Matrix.)

Territoriality Exercises

Changing Seats. One exercise which can be useful in understanding territoriality behavior is for leaders to ask a group that has been in session for a time (perhaps a half hour) to change seats. This can be done by asking the entire group to change places at once, or perhaps by going around the circle and asking each member in turn to select the place of another member (or leader) as his territory. After either approach, of course, members discuss the experience and the meaning it had for them. The continuums of dominance-submission, independence-dependence, competition-cooperation, the issues of aggression, timidity, authority figure perceptions, sex roles, the size of each member's life space are only a few of the possibilities for discussion. A word of caution: the leader should not feel it is necessary to introduce the above topics; rather, members should verbalize their reactions to the experience with the leader helping them see the meanings of their behaviors at whatever level seems appropriate for the maturity and psychological sophistication of the group.

(HIM Cells: The leader who is using the *Hill Interaction Matrix* as his cognitive map will note that the first version of this exercise encourages exploration at the Speculative levels in all cells, while the second exercise encourages interaction at the Confrontive levels in all cells.)

Drifting. Another exercise which involves territoriality is to ask members to drift about for an unspecified period of time. The leader deliberately avoids presenting any limits. Eventually each member will establish a "territory," either in subgroups or individually, standing or sitting. How long did this take? How did members feel standing about with no agenda? How did they structure their physical fields? How do they handle this situation in life outside the group? How do they handle time outside the group? How close did people stand together? Was this culturally determined?

(HIM Cell: On the HIM the exercise seems primarily directed at the "group" column and probably will explore the Speculative row.)

Feeling Space. A third exercise in the area of territoriality involves asking group members to close their eyes and explore the space about them while remaining seated and silent. They should be directed to feel down, back, up, to the side. Allow about three minutes for this. Leaders should keep their eyes open so that they can observe, making suggestions when necessary. At the end of the exercise discussion can center around members' reactions, especially those experienced when contact was made with another person—or was not made. How did members feel when they found someone else within their territory? How did they feel about temporary isolation from visual contact? How do they handle isolation elsewhere? What are their solitude needs? What are their companionship needs? How did they feel about making contact with a female? A male? The possibilities are infinite for discussion; the leaders must draw on their art of group leadership for direction.

(HIM Cell: The HIM Speculative, Personal and Relationship, will probably be the area of the Matrix tapped by this exercise.)

Break In. "Break In" is a standard verbal exercise used to illustrate and explore feelings of rejection and isolation. It also may be used nonverbally. Members are asked to stand in a tight circle and one person is left outside the circle. He attempts to penetrate the group in any way that he can. This exercise can become quite active, so appropriate precautions should be taken to insure safety. Although all members are aware that the experience is contrived, the person who experiences the isolation and rejection may be left with strong feelings, so leaders must be alert that ample opportunity is provided for discussion. The Break In can be used as a springboard for members to explore their feelings of being rejected, or "out group," by the current group or in their lives outside the group. The use of "territoriality" to define ingroup-outgroup lines can be explored. This is particularly helpful with students in a school setting.

(HIM Cell: The Assertive-Relationship and Personal probably will be tapped on the HIM by this exercise.)

Halfway Point. A moderately useful exercise is provided by asking a group to divide in half and have the two sections stand on either side of the room facing each other. Members are instructed that when they choose, and if they choose, they may walk out to the halfway point between the lines and wait for someone from the other side. When the two meet, whatever communication the two desire can take place, but communication is to be nonverbal. When all who wish have met another halfway, the group returns to their places and members verbalize their reactions to the experience, exploring their relationship with the persons who met them and those who did not.

(HIM Cell: This exercise may focus on Assertive-Personal, and

Assertive-Relationship, or may focus on Confrontive-Relationship.)

Danish Thumb Wrestle. The Danish Thumb Wrestle is useful when leaders feel that hidden aggressions and hostilities might be explored nonverbally. This may involve the entire group or only two members. Those involved form dyads, interlace their fingers, and hook thumbs, using one hand only. One person then attempts to force the thumb of the other person down for a count of three by applying pressure on his thumb. The discussion which follows should uncover any feelings of animosity between or among members which may have been hidden.

(HIM Cell: The exercise dwells mainly on the Assertive-Relationship area of the HIM.)

Distance Between Dyads. A helpful exercise to assist group members in experiencing their invisible territoriality boundaries, particularly as they may change from person to person, is to ask two members to stand across the room from each other, inside the inner edge of the group. One walks to the other until physical contact is made, then backs off until he finds a comfortable distance. This distance is carefully measured. Then the other member of the dyad executes the exercise and this distance is measured. Discussion can center around differences in the distances at which members are comfortable with each other and insight gained into each one's tolerance for closeness with others.

(HIM Cell: This exercise can tap the most productive cell of the Matrix—the Confrontive-Relationship Cell.)

SUMMARY

These comments have focused upon two related aspects of nonverbal behavior in groups—observing it and experiencing it. Both observations and experiences have been divided into body language and territorality. The inherent ambiguity of nonverbal messages has been stressed and the need for verbally checking out nonverbal messages through feedback has been emphasized.

The various nonverbal confrontation techniques which have been presented have included suggestions as to when and under what circumstances leaders might choose to use them as catalysts. The areas of the *Hill Interaction Matrix* where the exercises might fall have been identified. The importance of members verbally translating the feelings generated through these exercises by means of discussions has been stressed.

BIBLIOGRAPHY

Beier, E. *The Silent Language of Psychotherapy.* Chicago: Aldine Publishing Co., 1966.

Berger, Milton M., ed. *Videotape Techniques in Psychiatric Training and Treatment.* New York: Brunner/Mazel, 1970.

Berne, Eric. *Transactional Analysis.* New York: Grove Press, 1961.

Cullen, L. F. "Nonverbal Communication: An Exploratory Study." Unpublished Ed.D. Dissertation, U.S.C., 1966.

Devi, Indra. *Yoga for Americans.* Englewood Cliffs, N.J.: Prentice-Hall, 1959.

Ekman, P., and Friesen, W. "Nonverbal Behavior in Psychotherapy Research." *Research in Psychotherapy,* Vol. 3, Washington, D.C.: American Psychological Association, 1968.

Hall, E. *The Silent Language.* Garden City, N.Y.: Doubleday, 1959.

Hill, Wm. F. *HIM Hill Interaction Matrix.* Los Angeles: Youth Studies Center, U.S.C., 1965.

Mahl, G. "Gestures and Body Movements in Interviews." *Research in Psychotherapy,* Washington, D.C.: American Psychological Association, 1968.

Mehrabian, A. "Communication Without Words." *Psychology Today,* Vol. 2, 1968, pp. 52-55.

Psychology Today, Communications/Research/Machines Inc., Carmel Valley Road, Del Mar, Ca. 92014, Published monthly.

Schutz, William C. *Joy.* New York: Grove Press, 1967.

CHAPTER 9

THE USE OF VIDEOTAPE CONFRONTATION IN THE EXTENSIONAL GROUP: A DIALOGUE WITH SELF

- The Theory
- The Technique
- Summary
- Bibliography

To the Group Leader:

Any procedure you use in group work should be grounded in theory. The use of videotape is no exception. This chapter attempts to equip you as a group catalyst with both the technique and the theory of the use of videotape as a vehicle for confrontation with self.

CHAPTER 9

THE USE OF VIDEOTAPE CONFRONTATION IN THE EXTENSIONAL GROUP: A DIALOGUE WITH SELF

THE THEORY

A complete confrontation with self operating in natural habitat is a rare experience. Videotape recordings of existent group interactions allow for a walk into one's self in a way not available through any other media—human or nonhuman. The Blind Area (Cell II) of the Johari Window—Not known to me; Known to others—is clearly reflected by the video camera. The playback of the recording allows for an intense experience in the Personal-Confrontive Cell of the *Hill Interaction Matrix* in a depth not available in any other way.

Who am I? Before I can know, I must interact with another human who experiences me and "in an act of grace" gives me his feedback concerning that experiencing. Inevitably there is a heavy overlay of the other's biases, distortions, and values in the feedback no matter how earnest the attempt to be honest. How unique is the experiencing of interaction with another human—one's videotaped self—who can enter into dialogue with a minimum of divergent biases, distortions, and values. I define myself as I choose; I make my statements that "This is Man according to me," but at times I am hazy as to just what is contained in my self-definitions. When I meet myself face-to-face on video I can clear up discrepancies and more clearly understand the statements I am making—those which are in harmony with the human I want to be and those which are in disharmony. At that point I possess, probably for the first time in such depth, ammunition of change. Aware of contradictions between behaviors and values, I can change the behavior or change the value, if I choose. My presumed priorities which are not demonstrated in my actions can be reexamined and perhaps reordered. My dialogue with self through video tape offers me an opportunity to become authentic in my statements of my Essence. The specificity of the content of the videotape confrontation allows me to identify precisely areas I might wish to modify. For example, I might have had a vague idea that I wished I could be received by others as more open, but I had no specific behavior in mind which could be adjusted—I just wanted to be more open, period. Then, through a confrontation with self on videotape, I saw that I could unfold my arms from across my chest, sustain more fully direct eye contact, and refrain from covering my mouth with my hands as I listened. My body language had been sending a message of "closed system" while my self statement was "open system." Once I knew specifically the behaviors I wanted to change, the process fo projecting an authentic self was simplified. Only through video tape could I have learned of the contradictions existing so clearly between my inner self perceptions and my outer self projections.

Some behaviors I discovered in my dialogue with self I did not want to change, such as a tendency to hold my head in my hands when I was listening intently. I knew this projected a closed system, but it seemed authentic to me, and I was comfortable with this behavior. I noticed I tapped my foot when I was tense and this I did not wish to change. The action seemed to me to make an authentic statement. If others found it irritating, that had to be and was okay. Tapping my foot under tension was a statement I wanted to make. That is where I was at that time and the message was "straight."

It is true that I could view myself on videotape outside a group setting, but confronting myself as I interact with others provides a much more viable dialogue with self. The process of seeing myself on video and reflectively experiencing meaningful interaction with myself and with others helps me hear what others are saying to me in a way I had never been able to experience before. I can alter expectations I have of myself and of others as I encounter myself and others through videotape. Since my statements as to who I am are made through my actions, not through what I intend to do or wished I had done, I need to be aware of what those actions really are, especially as I interact with others in a group setting. My sense of identity can be clarified or even created. As I define my essence, I can get feedback for my dialogue with self through personal confrontation on videotape.

144

THE TECHNIQUE

A closed-circuit TV system provides the basic tool. Equipment should include a wide-angle lens, a closeup lens, and preferably two cameras. If equipment, except for the cameras, can be housed in another room, the sound distraction will be minimized. It is possible to shoot through a one-way glass if the lighting is adequate. There are a variety of cameras, recorders, and monitors available, ranging from under $500 to many thousands. Small, portable units will soon be available in color.

While the equipment is important, far more important is the skill of the person operating the camera. He must be sensitive to nonverbal communication within a group, and, if he is familiar with the group process itself, his astuteness will be enhanced. The entire videotape process will be only as good as the man behind the camera; thus it is recommended that initially a co-leader operate the equipment. This has the advantage of keeping the privacy of the group intact and places behind the lens a skilled group process observer who will focus on the listeners as frequently as on the speaker. After some experience group members also may wish to take turns being the cameraman. As each focuses the camera, he inevitably heightens his sensitivity to the multi-level communication channels flowing within the group.

Before videotaping is introduced leaders should clarify the purposes of using the media, and if members do not want to participate, obviously they should not be forced to do so. The initial recording session should be short in length with immediate playback so that group members can become accustomed to the process. At first they probably will tend to be self-conscious, but soon the novelty wears off and eventually members come to use the tool as a means to dialogue with self in relation to self, in relation to others, and in relation to situations and issues.

After the initial playback, future tapings may be more lengthy, but in all cases there should be opportunity for playback during the session in which the recording was made. The playback should be stopped frequently to allow for discussion, and members should have the absolute right to request instant replay at any time during a session. It is easy to lose sight of the fact that the consequent reaction and interaction to the tape is the primary purpose of the experience, not the tape record itself. The leader should bear in mind that it is during a member's verbalization of a value, attitude, or perception to people who are truly listening that he clarifies his outlook for himself. Talking at oneself in a mirror is singularly ineffective. Somehow we need others to hear us in order to understand ourselves and know who we are. Thus, when using videotape feedback, the consequent verbalizations are the important content, not the entertainment value of the tape. To gain maximum catalytic value from a tape, the leader may choose to run it through several times—both with and without sound.

A leader might assist members to react to themselves on tape by the use of incomplete sentence stems which each completes during the viewing. A leader will want to create his own, but suggestions might be:

1. I was pleased by . . .
2. I was startled by . . .
3. I liked . . .
4. Other people . . .
5. I would not like to change . . .
6. I would like to change . . .
7. My verbal messages . . .
8. My nonverbal messages . . .
9. I experienced . . .
10. I am feeling . . .

Possible insights gained from the dialogue with self through video-tape confrontation and through the incomplete sentences exercises might include an understanding of contradictory verbal and non-verbal messages a member is sending. Whether he wishes to change this behavior will, of course, be up to him, but a leader can help a member gain awareness of the dissonance. A member also might become aware of his characteristic defenses—perhaps intellectualization, or rationalization, or whatever. A member also may come to realize he is authority-figure-bound to a greater extent than he might wish. Projections come through loud and clear on video and members may be totally unaware that they were exhibiting these behaviors. The "taxes" (i.e., prescriptions for others' behaviors) placed on others in a thousand subtle ways may be recorded by the camera as it focuses on members who may wish to maintain tax-free relationships and have in fact believed they were doing so.

Members will probably experience increased caring for each other as a result of viewing video playback. During the initial interaction each was on "full force," while the playback session provides a reflective, feeling experience—a floating rather than a driving climate. Members can gain a profound awareness of their characteristic life

146

styles of being and relating. Self-defeating patterns of behavior may be identified. A member may gain an identification and acceptance of his physical self and may indeed come to love himself as his neighbor. In Harris's (1967) terms he may accelerate his ability to gain and to maintain an "I'm Okay, You're Okay" stance rather than remain in his "I'm Not Okay, You're Okay" trap. Incidentally, for leaders who wish to explore Berne's (1961) parent-child-adult ego states with a group, video recordings offer an excellent source of material relative to ego state and body posture.

Berger (1970) suggests that the spelling out of the anatomy of an attitude can be gained through videotape recordings. He pointed out that attitudes are composed of a variety of individual actions which include facial expressions, body stance, hand gestures, and characteristic mannerisms, and these actions can be identified as they transmit a particular attitude. For example, a person might find other group members experiencing him as judgmental, but not realize that his attitude is being transmitted through a facial expression and a rigidly held torso until he views himself on tape. A person may not be aware how she is coming on "little girl" until she views the sideways tilt of her head and her questioning speech pattern.

Students in the school setting can make excellent use of videotape for any of the above purposes. One of their major developmental tasks is to gain a sense of identity and increase their acceptance of selves and others; both of these objectives can be facilitated through the use of the video camera and playback monitor.

SUMMARY

The theoretical foundation based on an existential point of view which provides a rationale for the use of videotape as a means of personal confrontation—a dialogue with self—has been presented. Following it was a discussion of the techniques involved and the objectives which might indicate the use of this technique.

BIBLIOGRAPHY

Berger, Milton M., ed. *Videotape Techniques in Psychiatric Training and Treatment.* New York: Brunner/Mazel, 1970.

147

Group Leadership

Berne, Eric. *Transactional Analysis.* New York: Grove Press, 1961.

Harris, Thomas. *I'm Okay, You're Okay.* New York: Harper & Row, 1967.

Stoller, F. H. "The Long Weekend." *Psychology Today,* 1:28-33, 1967.

CHAPTER 10

SOME PRACTICAL CONSIDERATIONS IN ORGANIZING GROUPS IN PUBLIC SCHOOLS

- Does Group Counseling Belong In Public Schools?
- Staff Preparation
- Selection of Students
- Number of Sessions
- Logistics
- Suggested Group Formats
    - Format 1: Guidance Group
    - Format 2: Group Counseling with Pregroup Interview
    - Format 3: Group Counseling with no Interview
- Bibliography

To the Group Leader:

Getting organized may generate impatience on your part but the careful foundation you build for group life will insure a viable experience for your group members.

CHAPTER 10

SOME PRACTICAL CONSIDERATIONS IN ORGANIZING GROUPS IN PUBLIC SCHOOLS

A group is only as good as its leader. The leader is only as good as the care he exercises in organizing a group. This chapter addresses some practical details which leaders might wish to consider when organizing group counseling in public schools.

DOES GROUP COUNSELING BELONG IN PUBLIC SCHOOLS?

The educational goals which can be achieved though the use of group counseling in public schools are a legitimate concern of school counselors. Bates (1968) conducted research to identify which of those goals could be achieved through group processes when working with adolescents in a high school setting. According to her study, group counseling could be used to assist students to become more receptive to the learning process through a reduction of tensions and hostilities. In one of the group formats of this study, students were helped to maintain a grade point average, improve behaviors in the classroom, demonstrate more applied effort, and increase daily attendance. Students in the groups expanded the occupational choices into which they projected themselves, and these chosen occupations were more realistic when assessed against the students' academic potential. Group participants came to feel they were of more value to themselves, were more self-accepting, and were more aware of themselves as unique persons. They also came to place more value on others and became more aware of the universality of human experiences.

The goals and objectives which can be achieved through group counseling apparently are consonant with goals and objectives of education. In the Extensional model, counselors will assist prospective group members to identify those goals and objectives that each wishes to achieve. It is the counselor's responsibility to be knowledge-able concerning group research so that he can help a member identify achievable, realistic objectives. A chapter is provided in this manual discussing measuring instruments which might be used on an individual basis to gather data concerning the effectiveness of group work in achieving individual objectives.

STAFF PREPARATION

It is doubtful if other institutions experience quite the same degree of misunderstanding of the purpose of groups as is shown in the typical public school. The counselor who wishes to initiate group counseling may find time spent in staff preparation well spent. Without the staff's understanding and support almost any group counseling program will encounter difficulty.

First of all, the support of the administrators *must* be obtained—not just permission, but support, preferably enthusiastic support. If an administrator gives only lukewarm agreement, counselors may want to delay the group counseling program until such time as they are able to elicit clearer understandings on the part of administrators of the educational advantages of a group counseling program.

Once the support of the administration has been made clear, a general presentation concerning the nature of group counseling, its values and educational components, should be made to the faculty. At this point it is recommended that the building administrator verbalize support of the group counseling program to the entire faculty.

SELECTION OF STUDENTS

The best group member is a self-referred group member; group counseling should be optional for participants. Counselors will find that after a program of group counseling has been carried on for a semester or so, students will voluntarily request group counseling. Until they are familiar with the experience, however, the counselor may need to arrange some orientation directed at the entire student body. The authors of this book suggest that the counselor might go to classrooms and contact all students through a general guidance presentation, using the pamphlet provided in Appendix E, *So You Are Going To Be in Group Counseling.* Students should not be asked to volunteer for counseling groups at the time of the group guidance presentation. Rather, the counselor should suggest that students who are interested see him personally.

Once the counselor has eight to twelve students who wish to be in a group, he can begin to organize. It is the position of the writers that homogeneous groups are a myth, and that organizing a group around some "common problem" is not functional. All group members are homogeneous in that they are all unique human beings, each an individual unlike any other individual who has ever lived or ever will live. The notion that a group with "attendance problems" or "behavior problems" has a common problem is likely to be erroneous. If there are eight students whom the school has labeled "students with attendance problems," the etiology of the attendance problem of each of the eight will probably be quite different. Groups organized around a school problem are appropriately guidance groups, and counselors should not use them to seduce students into becoming counseling groups.

The writers suggest that for their first groups counselors attempt to restrict group membership to students of not more than two grade levels; developmental levels may be so different that group progress is hampered if students are too widespread in age. Another suggestion is that beginning group counselors work with students of one sex for their first group, as this will be easier to handle; coeducational groups are preferred once the counselor gains experience. In composing a counseling group counselors should take into consideration the degree to which each of the participants is verbal, as too few or too many highly verbal members may inhibit group interaction.

NUMBER OF SESSIONS

It is suggested that a counselor schedule a pre-group interview, eight group counseling sessions, and a post-group interview. Thus a counseling group can be organized, conducted, and evaluated within the framework of a school quarter. If the pre-group interview is done well, and if the group leaders are skilled, eight sessions should be productive. The notion of continuing one group for a semester or a year (or two!) in the public school setting is neither necessary nor even desirable in the opinion of the writers.

If a counselor feels an individual group member should continue working in a group, the member can be reassigned, and thus not be denied the opportunity for continuance. At the same time, each of the group members will have had the experience of working with a limited number of sessions and may have internalized a basic fact of living—that opportunities (and life) are limited.

LOGISTICS

If possible, a group should meet in other than a classroom setting. Privacy should be maximum, with *no* interruptions permitted. Chairs should be arranged in a circle but not around a table, since nonverbal communication involves the entire body.

The leader must begin on time, even if only one member is present; he also must end on time. Beginning group leaders tend to want to extend the time of their sessions, as groups led by beginners characteristically get down to work toward the end of a session. If neophyte leaders allow the time to be extended they are denying group members the opportunity to learn limits, and thus to gain experience in reality testing.

Usually the group meets weekly for one class period, although for very young children this schedule may be varied. It is better to meet for the same period each week, but if the group counselor works in a traditionally scheduled school, he may elect to rotate the periods for group meeting. In a modular scheduled school groups can meet when the student has free time, but it is suggested that no groups be organized before or after school or during the lunch hour. If counseling is a legitimate part of the educational program, then time ought to be available for group counseling as well as classroom instruction.

Check Sheet. This checklist for organizing the group might be useful as a quick reference.

CHECK SHEET FOR ORGANIZING A COUNSELING GROUP IN SCHOOLS

	Yes	No
1. Did you clear with administration and faculty?	☐	☐

2. Have you selected from eight to twelve potential members? ☐ ☐
3. Have you made a general presentation to students in the classroom setting? (optional) ☐ ☐
4. If this is your first group, are they all one sex? ☐ ☐
5. Is there no more than two years age span in students? ☐ ☐
6. Did you interview each one individually? ☐ ☐
7. Were you and each group member able to specify objectives in the pre-group interview? ☐ ☐
8. Did you explain each counselee's membership responsibility clearly? ☐ ☐
9. Did you locate some place in which to meet where you will have uninterrupted privacy? ☐ ☐
10. Did you clearly communicate time limits and number of sessions? ☐ ☐
11. Have you planned a post-group session with individual members to discuss their objectives? ☐ ☐

SUGGESTED GROUP FORMATS

Each group member is unique. Each group leader is unique. The extraordinary qualities of individual members and individual leaders make each group to some degree unpredictable. The complexities which comprise the entity called "group" are so intricate that they defy definition and, therefore, anticipation. Experienced and inexperienced leaders alike approach each group as an unknown. Perhaps a major difference between the experienced leader and the inexperienced leader is that the former knows he can never be sure what will evolve in a group and the latter still believes that, in time, he might.

The suggestions which follow, therefore, are presented as a skeletal framework to which the leaders must give the substance of life. Variations are infinite; the formats advanced below are only a benchmark, only the sketch of an outline. The intent is to provide a simplistic reference point from which leaders can move creatively into the intricacies of the group process.

Group Leadership

Format 1: Guidance Group

Situation: Counselor organizes guidance group for enculturating, e.g., referrals, "failure" notices, attendance problems, leadership development, etc.

Procedure: 1. Counselor pre-selects group.
2. Counselor interviews each member individually, asks that the student join if he wishes (optional step).
3. Three or four sessions, eight to twenty members.
4. Focus on Conventional level of HIM, some on Speculative.
5. Post-group interview optional. Assessment made on group basis, counselor selects instrument according to *his* objectives.

Format 2: Group Counseling with Pregroup Interview

Counselors initiate group counseling program in schools, K-12. Counselor makes group guidance presentation in classroom, using pamphlet *So You Are Going To Be In Group Counseling.* Covers responsibilities of group membership, limits of the group, such as number of sessions, size, areas to be explored, and what members *might* get out of the experience. Counselor discusses Johari Window. Asks students who wish to join a counseling group to see him in his office. Counselor avoids using group pressure to stimulate individual interest so he does not ask students to indicate an interest in joining a counseling group while he is making his group guidance presentation.

Situation: 1. Co-counselors obtain group leadership skills.
2. Consult with administration, informing them of procedures, objectives, and benefits of the group counseling program.
3. With support of administration, inform faculty; if possible, parents, and school board members.

Procedure: 1. Pregroup, individual interview of selected participants. (Those who cannot be placed in a group at this time are contacted and placed on a "wait" list.) Individual objectives identified and written on a 3 x 5 card.

2. Eight sessions held—one class period for junior high, high school, college, ½ hour for elementary school students, about 20 minutes for primary school students with each session "capped."

3. Postgroup interview, assessing objectives—no implication transmitted to counselee by counselor that gains made by end of session need be those set as objectives at beginning of sessions.

4. If counselor feels a member needs to continue, offer is made to place him in another group.

Possible catalytic techniques of session:

    (These suggestions are only that—an infinite variety should be created by the leaders.)

Session 1—Use mild confrontation technique, such as "Presentation of Other." (See material on Catalysts to Interaction.)

Session 2—Perhaps "New Names" or "Symbolic Objects" to begin interaction—respond to values, priorities, concepts of self.

Session 3—Perhaps no technique—group may begin self and counselors should avoid having participants become dependent on them to begin interaction.

Session 4—Ask if anyone wants to begin or if group wishes one of the leaders to begin interaction. May use "Magic Shop," "Territoriality," "Three Adjectives," etc.—probably a moderate technique.

Session 5—Same as above, if technique used may consider "Presentation of Self: Clothes," or "Taking A Trip."

Session 6—If technique is desired may use "Legitimizing," "Mirror Image," "First Impressions," etc.

Session 7—May want to use a nonverbal if appropriate, or "Strength Bombardment."

Session 8—No technique, or may ask members to respond to, "As a group member, I. . . . " Tie up loose ends. Be sure to have a "go around" during this session so each participant has an opportunity to verbalize unfinished business.

Format 3: Group Counseling with no Interview

Same as above, except if pre-group interview not feasible, use first session of group to *teach* group membership, talking about and practicing feedback; present Johari Window, Group Counseling pamphlet. Do not begin group interaction until Session 2.

BIBLIOGRAPHY

Bates, Marilyn. "A Test of Group Counseling." *Personnel and Guidance Journal,* April, 1968, pp. 749-53.

CHAPTER 11

ELEMENTARY SCHOOL GROUP COUNSELING

- Special Problems of Elementary School Counseling
  Groups
- A Consideration of Communication Patterns
- Resource Materials
  - Classroom Discussion Groups
  - Specialized Approaches to Elementary School
    Counseling Groups
- Bibliography

To the Group Leader:

Group counseling with elementary school students is different in some ways from counseling with other groups. Similarities and differences are pointed out in this chapter.

CHAPTER 11

ELEMENTARY SCHOOL GROUP COUNSELING

Group counseling with elementary school age children is, in essence, no different from counseling in groups with participants of any age. The Extensional Group model is appropriate for any group leader who is working with members who want to extend their abilities to function in the world, whether the members are students of elementary school age, secondary school age, or not students at all. There are, however, some special considerations which might be given to groups composed of elementary school age participants.

SPECIAL PROBLEMS OF ELEMENTARY SCHOOL COUNSELING GROUPS

In an elementary school age counseling group there are some special problems which are not likely to occur with older group members. The importance of preserving the integrity of the home and family is vital and the leader must be very alert that the young student does not discuss concerns which would violate this privacy. Elementary school children cannot be expected to have the degree of social sophistication which older students will have; thus, their privacy and their family's must be "protected" vigorously by group leaders. This may involve more frequent intervention on the part of the leaders than would be necessary when working with an older group.

Leaders of elementary school counseling groups need to observe some important parameters which are derived from the developmental age of these young students. Redl (1966) offers the suggestion that the way a counseling group of children is put together must not be left to chance, for the composition of group membership may be of great importance for the kind of group life which will develop and the effects the group will have on its members. In working with

161

students of this age bracket, the possibilities of contagion are greater than when students are older; therefore, children ought not be put into a group where they do not belong, because they will either seriously disturb the group or because they will suffer damage through exposure to the wrong group life. Redl feels that students should not be too far removed from one another in terms of toughness, physical prowess, sex sophistication, and developmental stage. If a leader finds that a student has been misplaced in a counseling group, he must confer with that student privately and remove him from the group.

Redl's life-space interview (1959) is directed toward work on an individual basis, but the goals which he specifies for the single interview are applicable to the goals of group counseling with elementary school children. Through the group process students can, in Redl's terms, experience a reality "rub-in" which will help youngsters who habitually misinterpret interpersonal situations (e.g., those who think the teacher is always "against" them) derive more appropriate meanings from social situations. Through group interaction students can come to see that a maladaptive style of life really involves more secondary pains than secondary gains. Through group a child can learn other ways of behaving which are satisfying and can expand psychological boundaries to include other adults and teachers and also include with acceptance aspects of himself which were formerly unacceptable. Redl (1959) identifies aspects of emotional first aid which also have relevancy to the group process in elementary schools. The group process can drain off hostilities and daily frustrations so as to prevent an intolerable accumulation; provide emotional support when children are overwhelmed by feelings of panic or guilt; provide a relationship which keeps the child from retreating into his own world as a consequence of emotional upheaval, govern social traffic so as to remind pupils of "house" policies and regulations; and finally, serve as a place to work out feelings concerning disputes, fights, and other "loaded transactions."

That there are some special considerations which must be observed when organizing and conducting groups composed of elementary school children is clear. The size of the group and the length of each session depends on the ages of the children; for example, in early childhood (ages five through nine) there should be only three to four members, carefully selected so as not to have more than one aggressive child and not more than one very passive child in the group. The process and content of the elementary school group also may differ from other groups, for example, the use of puppets, clay, art media; or the use of frequent role-playing, open-ended stories, and sociodrama.

Pre-adolescent groups (ages nine to thirteen) generally require less use of manipulative materials but the interaction may need to be facilitated by some activities. These children enjoy small groups composed of members of the same sex and game activities of interaction and expression. The activity allows members numerous opportunities for learning and practicing coping behaviors with peers of the same sex and age. Time is scheduled after each activity to permit members and the leader to discuss behavior elicited during the activity. Participation in the after-activity counseling group, of course, must be on a volunteer basis and the purpose of the discussion made very clear to members.

It is especially true that children during the early childhood and preadolescent ages need adult models of the same sex after which to pattern their lives, and this obviously has application to group counseling in elementary schools. The person of the leader provides a model, whether of the same or the opposite sex. Part of the content of these groups should be to bring into awareness the process and the importance of modeling.

Leaders who work with elementary school groups will find that they must do more "teaching" through a direct approach of listening skills, membership skills, and individual behaviors than would be necessary or desirable in older age groups. Children will need a great deal of help in labeling emotions as well as articulating their value systems. Positive emotional development in children is analogous to self-actualization in adults (Tillinghast, Jr., 1970) and leaders of elementary school counseling groups can make provision through the group process to insure that children experience joy as valuable in itself.

A CONSIDERATION OF COMMUNICATION PATTERNS

The group leader who works from an Existentialist framework and who is working with the Extensional model will find that the principles and procedures of enhancing communication which are advanced in this manual are appropriate when working with groups of all ages. The pre-group interview, the eight-session format, the post-group interview, the setting of individual specific objectives, are all just as functional with elementary school children as with older participants. There will be limitations, however, which the group leader will experience in working with students this age. One will be the length of the session. For primary school children sessions of from fifteen to twenty minutes in length will provide ample time for group work; also for these children, a very small group is desirable—from three to five has usually worked out well. (The use of videotape is an excellent tool and one to which children this age respond readily.)

Children of elementary school age will not be as practiced at verbalizing feelings as older students are. Even more than older students they probably tend to respond with "It" type comments, i.e., facts, events, things away from the group which deal with the "there and then." They also will tend to make "They" responses, that is, focus on people away from the group rather than deal with each other. Thus, young students will need help in communicating. A leader might be alert to types of responses and may either model more productive interaction or discuss interaction patterns directly.

Students probably will tend to "chain" at first, i.e., respond to one another's comments with replies which indicate no verbalized recognition of the content of the other's remarks. For example, a group member might state that he had had a bad night's sleep. A chaining response might be "I just got a new spread for the bed in my bedroom. It's really neat!" This type of response chains to the output, but gives the original speaker no indication that his comment held meaning for the receiver. Students of all ages, but particularly those of elementary school age, need to be helped to make associative rather than chaining responses.

In the associative response the hearer gives some recognition that he has heard the speaker, but centers his response egocentrically. When a group member comments about his bad night's sleep, the associative responder might reply, "Yeah, I know what you mean. I really had a rough night, too. I'm beat today." While this type of response leaves the original speaker with some small degree of satisfaction, he receives only a minimal amount of feedback from the verbalization. He was heard, but he does not know if he was understood.

A group counselor can, through modeling, teach students to give feedback types of responses. These require a high degree of listening skills on the part of students, but this is one of the functions of the group process—to help students learn to listen to each other. The feedback level of response centers on what the speaker is saying, responds to it, and enriches it. To illustrate, in responding to the bad night's sleep comment, a feedback response might be, "You seem kind of tired. It is kind of difficult to get along without enough sleep." The speaker knows that he has been heard, he knows that he has been understood, and he knows that his feelings are recognized. All group participants will have some difficulty in learning to give this sort of feedback, but elementary school students will have a particular struggle in learning how to communicate at a level where they transmit "hearing" feelings and unverbalized messages.

RESOURCE MATERIALS

McCarty's (1969) *It All Has To Do With Identity* has been reviewed in the appendix and the group counselor who works with elementary school children might wish to refer to this tool which is designed to "teach" the group process to students this age. There are a number of other resource materials which may prove useful when working with elementary school age children. The reader is provided with a general description of content in the following comments, but is urged to contact the bibliographic source for the original materials if interested in further information.

Classroom Discussion Groups

The reflection of a guidance point of view is demonstrated by the several excellent methods designed to help the classroom teacher conduct discussion groups composed of elementary school children: Glasser's (1969) classroom meeting, Dreikurs' (1968) group discussions, and Randolph's (1968) *SEE*. Professionals who have expertise in group processes ought to be prepared to help the classroom teacher to organize, conduct, and evaluate such groups. The trained group

165

leader can and should serve as consultant in group dynamics to the teacher. The trained group leader should be familiar with recent group approaches to classroom interaction groups, but it is beyond the scope of this book to describe these approaches in detail, and the reader is referred to the original sources provided in the bibliography at the end of this chapter. Strickland and Engemoen (1968) have written a pamphlet entitled, *The Counselor as a Resource Person to Elementary School Teachers: Rationale and Methodology*, which provides direction to the counselor who will be working with the elementary school teacher in group work and with individual students.

Specialized Approaches to Elementary School Counseling Groups

Although the literature specifically addressed to the counselor who works with elementary school age groups is limited, there are several approaches described below which might be of interest to leaders who plan on working with the students of this age and situation. The initial one is a handbook issued by the Los Angeles Schools specifically aimed at pupil personnel workers who deal with elementary school counseling groups. The second is a behavioral approach to group counseling with children, followed by an Existential, Here and Now approach. A discussion of an activity group approach precedes a model which approaches the group process from the point of view of developing each student's potential.

A Guide to Group Counseling in Elementary Schools (Los Angeles Unified School District, 1969) is a useful publication for elementary school group counselors. The handbook sees group counseling as being used to alleviate anxieties and emotional tensions, to resolve conflicts, to develop self-understanding, to facilitate the learning of acceptable, gratifying behavior, to assist in achieving maturity and increased sensitivity to the needs of others, and to help each student evaluate his own behavior. Suggestions concerning group interaction are followed by a discussion on how and when to terminate a group, concluding with evaluation methodology as it applies to the group counseling program.

166

A Cognitive-Behavioral Approach to Group Counseling with Children was developed by Mayer, Rohen, and Whitley (1969) as an approach to counseling with elementary school children which is based on a combination of dissonance theory with social learning theory. Mayer feels that group counseling offers an excellent environment for the creation of dissonance, since more than one model is provided for each student to listen to, observe, and interact with. Thus, contradictory items of information are likely to be available in the group. Positive reinforcement can be supplied both by group members and the leader.

A Reality-Here-and-Now Approach. Bigelow and Thorne compared two elementary school counseling groups, using the Hill Interaction Matrix as the instrumentation. The research design contrasted a group where the leader attempted to work at the Confrontation level on the HIM with a group where the leader assumed a non-directive stance. The sessions ran for six meetings. The group which received little intervention on the part of the counselor interacted at a significantly lower therapeutic level than did the confrontive group. At the end of the six sessions the group which focused on Hill's more productive level (Confrontation) showed significantly more productive interactions.

Activity Group Therapy. Another possible approach to group counseling with elementary school children is suggested by Charles King (Los Angeles County Schools Publication, Mimeographed, 1957). King's approach is geared to students between the ages of eight and fourteen, working in a group of like sex and numbering from five to eight. King's comments are addressed to groups which meet outside the public school setting, but his procedures could be adapted to the school situation. The "club" (group) meets in a room designed to permit a maximum range of physical activity— running, jumping, and chasing; provision is made for "retiring" corners. A round table and several smaller tables are essential, as are tools and materials which consist of very "easy" arts and crafts type resources. King emphasizes that the product in the club is never permitted to be an end in itself; rather, the process of creating and the emotional experiences of the process are the objective of the

167

activity. Food is seen as essential, and one of the strongest bonds in creating a sense of belonging to the group. The leader assumes a neutral and accepting role, but he provides a point of reality and reassuring authority to the group. He does not talk much, pushes group decisions back to the group wherever feasible, but is always available. King's activity group approach is almost totally non-interpretive; he sees the force of the process as lying in the dynamic acting-out between members of the group around the stable fulcrum of the leader. The activity group is aimed at enhancing, encouraging, and strengthening self-esteem, role-identification, and a capacity for relationships, both with peers and with adults.

Developing Human Potential. Otto (1970) has maintained consistently that "every student is a gifted student" and his suggestions concerning the developing of the elementary school student's potential contain an appropriate approach to group counseling with students of this age. Otto's stance is "life-affirmative" and follows the principles of: "Man is a continuous process of self-creation; Growth in life occurs through human relationship; Self-knowledge is the first step toward self-realization; Crisis is an opportunity for growth; Humor is the confident expression of a developing selfhood; The optimal use of communication is a requisite in developing human potential" (Otto, 1970: 133-166).

Otto feels strongly that, for an elementary pupil's potential to be enhanced, it is necessary to provide personal growth experiences for the teacher, who will then be more aware of the needs of the student and will have the ability to respond to these needs. Otto's program, "Human Potential Seminars," is reviewed in the appendix of this manual so his procedures will not be discussed here. The approach to emphasizing strengths, however, cannot be too strongly recommended to counselors who are working with groups of students in the public school setting—particularly the elementary school setting.

BIBLIOGRAPHY

Bigelow, Gordon S., and Thorne, John W. "Reality Versus Client-Centered Models in Group Counseling." *School Counselor,* Vol. 16, No. 3, Jan., 1969, pp. 194-95.

Dimick, Kenneth M., and Huff, Vaughn. *Child Counseling*. Dubuque, Iowa: Wm. C. Brown Co., 1970.

Dreikurs, B., and Grey, L. *Logical Consequences*: *A New Approach to Discipline*. New York: Meredith, 1968.

Glasser, William. *Schools Without Failure*. New York: Harper & Row, 1969.

Hill, Wm. Fawcett. *Hill Interaction Matrix*. Los Angeles: Youth Studies Center, University of Southern California, 1965.

King, Charles. "Activity Group Therapy," Mimeographed paper, Los Angeles County Superintendent of Schools, Division of Research and Pupil Personnel Services, #37511, January 1957.

Los Angeles Unified School District, "A Guide to Group Counseling in Elementary Schools," Division of Elementary Education, Guidance and Counseling Section, Revised, October 1969.

Mayer, G. Roy; Rohen, Terrence; and Whitley, A. Dan. "Group Counseling with Children," *Journal of Counseling Psychology*, Vol. 16, No. 2, 1969, pp. 124-149.

McCarty, Terry. *It All Has To Do With Identity*. Youth Studies Center, University of So. California, 1968.

Otto, Herbert A. "Developing Student Potential." *California Elementary Administrator*, Vol. 33, No. 4, May 1970, pp. 7-9.

Otto, Herbert A. *A Guide to Developing Your Potential*. North Hollywood: Wilshire Book Co., 1970.

Randolph, Norma, and Howe, Wm. *SEE*. Cupertino, Cal.; Cupertino School District, 1968.

Redl, F. "The Concept of the Life Space Interview." *American Journal of Orthopsychiatry*, 1959, Vol. 29, pp. 1-18.

Redl, F. *When We Deal With Children*. New York: Free Press, 1966.

Strickland, Ben, and Engemoen, Bonny. *The Counselor as A Resource Person to Elementary School Teachers*: *Rationale and Methodology*. Division of Guidance Services, Texas Education Agency, Austin, Texas, Jan. 1968.

Tillinghast, Jr., B.S. "Needed: A Psychology of Joy for Children." *Guidepost*, Vol. 12, No. 9, June 1970, p. 3. American Personnel and Guidance Association.

CHAPTER 12

MEASURING A MEMBER'S PROGRESS

- Theoretical Paradigms
- Research Design
- Assessment Tools
- Summary
- Bibliography

To the Group Leader:

You, as group leader, have the expertise to select appropriate instrumentation. You and each group member interact to define and assess individul objectives.

CHAPTER 12

MEASURING A MEMBER'S PROGRESS

During the pregroup interview leader and member meet together in privacy to discuss the member's fantasies concerning group membership and the group. At this time, the two also very specifically enumerate objectives the participant would like to achieve through his commitment to the group. The group leader is responsible for providing the tools to measure progress toward these objectives, and it is the purpose of this chapter to suggest to the leader tools which might be used. Leaders should consult published test lists for additional possibilities. This chapter begins with a theoretical model(s) against which progress may be measured, then presents in detail some specific measuring instruments as well as general suggestions.

THEORETICAL PARADIGMS

Before any instrumentation can be applied to progress as a result of group experience or any other treatment, the question must be answered, "Measured against what?" Some theoretical model must be specified if measurement is to have any meaning. The measuring tool can make an objective operational; the assumptions and constructs behind the tool make it meaningful.

Maslow's Model of Personality

Maslow's (1962) model of the self-actualizing person provides a framework which seems to the authors of this book to offer one satisfactory paradigm of what *man* can be and what *Man* can be. The reader is referred to Maslow's (ibid.) writings for thorough review, but briefly the self-actualizing person has these characteristics:

Compared to "normal" people he has a more efficient perception of reality and a more comfortable relationship with it. He has an ability to detect the fake and the flaws in people and things.

The ability to accept himself, other people, and nature as they are. He does not experience psychological guilt, anxiety, shame, chagrin. He is not defensive; enjoys living; does not pose.

Spontaneous behavior marked by simplicity and naturalness.

The focus is on world and cultural problems. In general, self-actualizing people have solved their personal problems and are addressing their energies to society's concerns.

A quality of detachment; he enjoys privacy.

Autonomous, he resists acculturation. He is also growth-motivated rather than deficiency-motivated.

A continuing freshness of appreciation. He finds richness in subjective experiences, and has rich emotional reactions.

A higher frequency of peak experiences.

Increased identification with the human species—he feels a basic kinship with people.

Deep and profound interpersonal relationships. Compared with "normal" people, he is capable of more perfect love and greater empathy. He tends to select friends who exhibit self-actualizing characteristics.

A high degree of creativeness.

A democratic character structure—being unaware of differences of social class, race, or color.

A value system is based on his acceptance of himself and others. He is simultaneously the most ethical, most moral, most lusty, and most animal of people.

If group leaders have in mind a model such as the above when they are conceptualizing "psychological health," and hope it will be facilitated through group experiences, some of the objectives they set with a potential group member might be: increased feelings of

174

zest in living; more serenity; more joy; more peace of mind; more taking of responsibility for one's own actions; more confidence in one's ability to handle stresses, anxieties, and problems. The feelings of self-betrayal; of living by fear rather than growth; feelings of anxiety, despair, boredom; inability to enjoy; intrinsic guilt; intrinsic shame; aimlessness; feelings of emptiness; lack of identity— these may diminish or disappear.

As a group leader and member define individual objectives which the member wishes to accomplish in group, both will find that some of the objectives can be evaluated only subjectively. Others can be evaluated more objectively, but, regardless of the subjectivity or objectivity of the final evaluation, it is important that both leader and member realize that the establishing of specific, carefully thought-through objectives is essential. The reaching of these objectives is important, but secondary to the goal-setting process which precedes the group experience.

Sensitivity to People

Another relevant conceptualization of what people *might* be, perhaps as a result of group interaction, is provided by Smith (1966) in his work on sensitivity. Smith defines sensitivity as the ability to predict what an individual will feel, say, and do about you, himself, and others. It is the ability to sense accurately what others think and feel. Smith has identified six components of sensitivity as follows: (1) The general tendency to make favorable/unfavorable ratings of others. The person who tends to rate people high is probably more sensitive. The person who tends to be a high rater of others also tends to be more considerate and more observant of them; (2) The variability a person introduces into his estimates of others. A person who "jumps to conclusions" about another tends to be less sensitive than one who suspends judgment and who changes easily from situation to situation; (3) The amount of accurate empathy a person feels and can communicate; (4) The accuracy of observation; (5) The ability to build accurate stereotypes; (6) Having a working model of personality traits.

Smith contended that these components of sensitivity can be taught and can be measured. The relevancy for group leaders is obvious, but as group leaders we cannot take for granted that members will choose to increase their sensitivity—or want to become self-actualizing. This decision is made by the group member in the induction session. The group leader's responsibility is to select the appropriate instrumentation.

RESEARCH DESIGN

For a group leader who is not concerned with rigorous research, the pre-group and the post-group assessment will be sufficient to accomplish his purpose—that of evaluating an individual member's progress. For the group leader who is concerned with gathering data which can be analyzed statistically, Campbell and Stanley's (1963) presentation of experimental designs offers an excellent resource. The perennial problem which has clouded the results of studies of the effectiveness of group work will need to be faced, however. *If* a group mean statistic is used, the basic stance that a group does not have a group goal, but only individual objectives for each individual member, is contradicted. What is gain for one group member may be a loss for others; therefore, a researcher in group process must be prepared to state individual hypotheses for each of his subjects if he is to remain consistent. The fact that this complicates research procedures is recognized, but the reader is referred to the abundant literature on groups in which different (desired) directions of movement of individual members cancelled out statistical significance. (See "Group Counseling," *Journal of Research and Development in Education* (1968) ; and "Research Reports of Evaluation of Group Counseling," P. Corrales-Diaz, May 1970.)

Notwithstanding the research problems of validity of self-report instruments, of contradictory but desirable individual trends cancelling out significance of statistical tests, of criterion problems—the fact remains that evidence has been gathered which indicates that achievable objectives *can* be specified, *can* be met, and *can* be measured (Bates, 1968) . The reader is also referred to the comprehensive bibliography of group procedures in guidance compiled by Zimpfer for the New York Personnel and Guidance Association (1969) .

ASSESSMENT TOOLS

As indicated in the introductory comments, this chapter presents selected assessment tools which group leaders may use to measure a member's movement toward his objectives. Each assessment tool presented below in alphabetical order is briefly described as to its possible use, and an indication given as to the age group for which the instrument was designed. Sources of further information and means of obtaining copies of the instruments are provided. A detailed bibliography is provided at the end of the chapter.

Allport-Vernon-Lindsay. *Study of Values* (1960)

This widely-known scale for measuring dominant values in personality has been abundantly researched. As a before-and-after measuring tool, however, it should be used with caution as the six measured values are not independent of one another and therefore statistical techniques must be used with care.

Bills, Robert E. *Index of Adjustment and Values*

Group leaders who wish to measure self-concept change, both in relation to self and to perceptions of others, may wish to consider the *Index of Adjustment and Values* (Bills, undated). This instrument is easy to score, has forms for elementary, junior high school, high school, and adult levels. It is thoroughly researched, with satisfactory reliability and validity data. It has been widely used as a measure of change through group experience. The reader may write to Robert E. Bills, School of Education, University of Alabama, for the instrument and manual, specifying the age level to be measured.

Coopersmith, Stanley. *Self-Esteem Inventory*

The *Self-Esteem Inventory* is directed toward children and designed to measure an individual's general appraisal of his worth, which Coopersmith (1967) claims remains stable over a period of several years. He also comments that people generally are unwilling to accept evidence that they are better or worse than they themselves have decided. The SEI is a fifty-item inventory, and the scales sort the items into two groups—those indicative of high self-esteem and those indicative of low self-esteem.

Coopersmith, who designed the instrument for his landmark study of the antecedents of self-esteem, does not report its use as a measure of change derived from group experience, but it may be found appropriate for group leaders who are looking for tools which can be used to measure these areas in elementary school children. Information can be obtained from Stanley Coopersmith, Associate Professor of Psychology, University of California, Davis, California.

Hill, Wm. F. *HIM-B*

The HIM-B consists of sixty-four items, four for each of the sixteen cells of the Matrix (the Responsive level is excluded). The test can be hand-scored or machine-scored. The results will provide a Total Acceptance Score of the group process, as well as information concerning an individual's preferential mode of functioning in the *Hill Interaction Matrix*. The instrument can be used as a pre- and post-measure of group movement, or can be used as a screening measure to match prospective group members to a specific group leader, or to assign members to a specific group. The instrument can be obtained from Dr. Hill at the Youth Studies Center, University of Southern California, Los Angeles.

Hill, Wm. F. *HIM-G*

The HIM-G is intended to rate a group session through use of a recording, videotape, or typescript of the session. Group movement from cell to cell of the HIM can be traced. Thus group leaders can obtain an assessment of the areas in which they actually worked.

Rating a group by the HIM-G requires specialized training, but protocols of sessions can be scored by raters trained by Hill. The reader is referred to Dr. Hill at the University of Southern California, Los Angeles, for cost and time involved.

O'Sullivan, M., et al.

O'Sullivan and Guilford (1965) have written a series of booklets which group leaders might find useful to measure the components of sensitivity similar to those suggested by Smith (1966). O'Sullivan et al. present pictures which depict relationships in a variety of ways. The material contains no written material, and thus is nonverbal.

These booklets may be obtained from the Sheridan Supply Co., Beverly Hills, Ca.

Pettus, W. *PAC-Index of Maturity*

The *PAC-Index of Maturity* uses Q-methodology in a measure of maturity which is based on Eric Berne's (1961) parent-adult-child model of personality. The instrument was designed specifically to measure any movement toward "maturity" (as defined by the PAC) which occurs as a result of group experience. The PAC is directed primarily toward adolescents.

The student is presented with a set of small cards (about 1" x 3") on which are written statements derived from a pool of statements gleaned from students' completions of Rotter's *Incomplete Sentences Blank* (1950). The student is asked to place each card in a "normal" curve, ranging from those which he would be "Least Likely to Say" to those he would be "Most Likely to Say." The card sort contains sixteen statements representing each of the three ego states: parent, adult, and child. Readers may obtain copies of the instrument and scoring directions from the writers of this manual.

Rokeach, Milton. *Value Survey*

Milton Rokeach (1967) has designed an instrument to measure two types of values—instrumental and terminal. The inventory has an exceptionally attractive format which makes the process of completing the survey a pleasant experience in itself. The time of administration is minimal, and a group leader who wishes to measure changes in value hierarchy may well consider this instrument.

Rotter, Julian B. *Incomplete Sentences Blank*

The *Rotter Incomplete Sentences Blank* (1950) is a semi-projective tool which generates a quantitative score. This score, acording to the author of the test, may serve as an index of maladjustment. Thus group leaders may wish to use the ISB as a screening instrument, but also the tool is helpful as a pre- and post-measure of growth in group. Copies of the instrument together with a scoring manual may be obtained from The Psychological Corporation, 304 E. 45th Street, New York, N.Y. 10017.

School Records. It is possible to use data from school records as assessment of progress in group, although group leaders and group members need to be realistic concerning the grossness of these ratings as well as their subjective nature. Higher or lower grade point averages may be an objective of a group member which he anticipates may occur as a result of his experience in groups. A more satisfactory "Citizenship" rating by the teacher may be a desired outcome. "Effort" grades may be another criterion. Attendance patterns, i.e., number of absences, may be observed, and perhaps used as a measure of progress. Number of referrals from teachers, number of extracurricular activities, number of completed assignments, number of self-referrals for counseling—all these may be appropriate for any one group member. A measure of study habits available for most grade levels also may be indicated.

Schutz, William. *FIRO-B and FIRO-F*

"FIRO-B" stands for Fundamental Interpersonal Relations Orientation—Behavior, and the purpose of the instrument is to measure how an individual characteristically relates to other people. Schutz postulates that people have three interpersonal needs areas which involve joy and misery—inclusion, control, and affection. The measure leads to six scores: expressed inclusion and wanted inclusion behavior, expressed control and wanted control behavior, expressed affection behavior and wanted affection behavior. For example, in measuring "Affection" FIRO-B includes a statement, "I act close and personal toward people," to measure expressed affection behavior, and "I want people to get close and personal with me" to measure wanted affection behavior.

The "FIRO-F" stands for Fundamental Interpersonal Relations Orientation—Feelings and is designed to measure a person's characteristic feelings towards others. The dimensions of the instrument are significance, competence, and lovability, and the instrument measures interaction as well as individual traits.

Schultz has other instruments derived from his theory of interpersonal behavior. He suggests that the FIRO-B is useful as a pre- and post-measure of group changes in interpersonal relations during and following group experiences. The instrument may be used with children and adults

FIRO materials may be obtained from the Consulting Psychologists Press, Inc., 577 College Ave., Palo Alto, Ca. 94307.

180

Shostrom, Everett L. *POI Personal Orientation Inventory*

The POI is based on Maslow's Self-Actualizing constructs. The inventory consists of pairs of statements and the respondent is asked to decide which of the two statements more consistently applies to him. The inventory contains 150 pairs of statements, and a separate answer sheet is designed to accompany the test booklet. Scoring stencils are required to hand-score the instrument, which can also be machine-scored. A profile sheet is generated which provides scores on a variety of dimensions, e.g., self-actualizing value, spontaneity, self-regard, acceptance of aggression, capacity for intimate contact, etc. The reader may contact Everett L. Shostrom, through the Educational and Industrial Testing Service, San Diego, Ca. 92107.

Tyler, Leona E. *Vocational Choice Cards*

These Vocational Choice Cards consist of a set of small (1" x 3") cards on which are typed fifty occupations which were chosen by one group of students as those vocations which most interested them. The student is asked to place each card into one of three categories: "Would Choose," "Would Not Choose," and "No Opinion." The cards were originally designed to be used in individual vocational exploration, but they have been adapted satisfactorily to group administration and serve as a useful measure of the degree to which students' vocational horizons have expanded as a result of group counseling (Bates 1968).

Group leaders who wish to measure group counseling in relation to vocational choice can administer the cards before and after. Students can sort the cards in an individual session, or can select their choices in a group situation. For the purposes of measuring the effectiveness of group counseling in expanding vocational horizons, the *number* of choices suffice as criteria. The mean difference between choices prior to group counseling and choices after group counseling can be tested for significance, using standard statistical procedures.

In groups where the Tyler cards have been used, and where a statistically significant difference in number of choices has been demonstrated, the subject of vocational choice was *not* introduced into the content of the group interaction by the leader. Apparently, as students gain more self-esteem and come to value themselves more through the group experience, they widen their vocational choices. Readers may write to Leona E. Tyler at the University of Oregon for more information, or request from the U.S. Office of Education. Co-operative Research Project No. 2455.

Winters, Walter. *Perception of Self*

The *Perception of Self* instrument (Winters 1966) is designed to identify students who are having the most difficulty negotiating the identity crisis. The instrument consists of fifty-two items to which the student can respond in a group-testing situation. The purpose of the inventory is to help a counselor identify students who need assistance with educational and vocational planning, but it can also be used as a screening tool for group counseling. Scoring the *Perception of Self* requires scoring stencils. The reader is referred to Dr. Walter Winters, Huntington Beach Union High School District, Huntington Beach, Ca., for permission to use the instrument and for scoring procedures.

SUMMARY

The leader and the group member must select objectives and instrumentation of those objectives on an individual basis, thus assessing progress on an individual basis. What may be gain for one group member might be regression for another. If a leader takes the position that there are no *group* goals but only *individual* objectives, then it follows that measuring the effectiveness of the group process in meeting the objectives of members *must* be done on an individual basis, with leader and member selecting those measuring tools appropriate to the idiosyncratic objective of each group member.

BIBLIOGRAPHY

Allport, Gordon; Vernon, Philip E.; and Lindzey, Gardner. *Study of Values.* 3rd ed. Boston: Houghton Mifflin, 1960.

Bates, Marilyn. "A Test of Group Counseling." *Personnel & Guidance Journal*, April 1968, pp. 749-753.

Bates, Marilyn. "Group Processes: A Mini Manual." Orange County Personnel & Guidance Association, Orange County, Ca. Department of Education, 1969.

Berne, Eric. *Transactional Analysis in Psychotherapy.* New York: Grove Press, 1961.

Bills, Robert E. "Index of Adjustment and Values." University of Alabama, Alabama, n.d.

Campbell, Donald T., and Stanley, Julian C. "Experimental and Quasi-Experimental Designs for Research on Teaching," edited by N.L. Gage in *Handbook of Research on Teaching* (American Educational Research Association, Rand McNally, 1963.)

Coopersmith, Stanley. *The Antecedents of Self-Esteem.* San Francisco: W. H. Freeman, 1967.

Coopersmith, Stanley. *Self Esteem Inventory (SEI)* —Write S. Coopersmith, Associate Professor of Psychology, University of California, Davis, Ca.

Corrales-Diaz, Patricia. "Research Report of Evaluation of Group Counseling." Los Angeles County Superintendent of Schools, Division of Research & Pupil Personnel Services, May 15, 1970, mimeographed.

"Group Counseling," *Journal of Research and Development in Education,* Vol. 1, #2, Winter, 1968, Athens, Georgia.

Hill, Wm. F. HIM-B & HIM-G, in *A Supplement to HIM Monograph."* n.d., University of Southern California, University Park, Youth Studies Center, Los Angeles 90007.

Maslow, Abraham H. *Toward A Psychology of Being,* 2nd ed. New York: Van Nostrand Reinhold, 1962.

O'Sullivan, Maureen, and Guilford, J. P., et al. *Expression Grouping, Picture Exchange, Cartoon Predictions, Faces, Missing Pictures.* Beverly Hills: Sheridan Supply Co., 1965.

Pettus, William F., "PAC: An Instrument Designed to Provide an Operational Definition of Maturity Based on Berne's Model of Personality." Unpublished Master's Project, California State College, Fullerton, June 1970.

Rokeach, Milton. *Value Survey.* Halgren Tests, 873 Persimmon Ave., Sunnyvale, Ca., 1967.

Rotter, Julian B. *Incomplete Sentences Blank.* Psychological Corporation, New York, 1950.

Schutz, William C. *The FIRO Scales.* Consulting Psychologists Press, 577 College Ave., Palo Alto, Ca. 94301.

183

Schutz, William C. *FIRO—A Three-Dimensional Theory of Interpersonal Behavior*. New York: Rinehart, 1958.

Shostrom, Everett L. *POI. Personal Orientation Inventory*. Educational and Industrial Testing Service, San Diego, Ca. 92107.

Smith, Henry Clay. *Sensitivity to People*. New York: McGraw-Hill, 1966.

Tyler, Leona E. *Vocational Choice Cards*. University of Oregon, Eugene, Ore., 1964.

Winters, Walter. *Perception of Self*, Unpublished inventory, Huntington Beach, California, 1966.

Zimpfer, David G. *Group Procedures in Guidance, A Bibliography*. Albany, N.Y.: New York State Personnel & Guidance Association, 1969.

CHAPTER 13

MISUSE OF GROUPS

To the Group Leader:

Groups are crucibles of intense emotional and intellectual experiences. These experiences can be nourishing or they can be toxic. Your leadership will determine the direction.

CHAPTER 13

MISUSE OF GROUPS

Group can be a good thing or a very bad thing. Group can be nourishing or toxic. The vigorous growth of the group movement attests to its potential value. Through group interactions people have been freed of nonfunctional behavior patterns, but people also have been hurt by the group process. Group is not a harmless toy which can be manipulated freely with no fear of negative consequence. The profession's growing concern over the misuse of groups is derived from experiences with leaderless groups, commercial exploitation of the group process, inappropriate parameters for public institution groups, and groups led by ill-prepared leaders who equate group membership with group leadership (Shepard and Lee, 1970; Shostrom, 1970; Stoller, 1970).

The authors of this book have specified minimal training standards for leaders of various types of groups in Appendix B. This chapter specifically addresses some current misuses of groups. Focus is on the dangers of inadequate group leadership, exploitation of group phenomena in the form of "parlor games" designed to entertain, and misuse of groups in public schools. Suggestions are presented for avoiding a toxic group.

THE LEADER AS A MISUSER OF GROUPS

The most flagrant misusers of groups are ill-prepared group leaders who apparently do not recognize that accepting responsibility for a group implies an ethical commitment to members to insure that they experience positive growth, that they find caring relationships, that they can place trust in the leadership, that their personal privacy will not be invaded, and that they find the process manipulated, not themselves.

Group Leadership

Many people with little or no supervised, formal training are leading groups today. Their preparation consists entirely of experience as a member of a group. These "leaders" have learned group jargon and talk glibly of honesty, awareness, emotional growth, feelings, contact, freedom, trust, and perhaps are able to transmit authentically as a person. They generally are well-intentioned, but apparently do not recognize that group leadership is quite different from group membership, and that the former requires a high degree of specific professional skill.

Professional groupers may have clocked in an impressive number of hours as group members. They have learned the topography and consider themselves experts—which they may well be—in group membership. Unfortunately, they often view group as an end in itself and see the group process as a source of psychological excitement, at times using it as a place to act out regressive behaviors. According to Howard (1970:33) "Such zealots are known to group leaders . . . as lab hounds, group freaks, or sensitivity heads. The hounds, freaks, and heads don't seem to have much of a social life outside the groups. They live—as it is possible to do, especially in California—from one group-generated spell of euphoria to the next, savoring the instant intimacy some groups are famous for providing. For these people it is old hat to leave matters of friendship, affection, and love to chance and chemistry." Perennial groupers seem to use their membership as a way of life, even as a sexual mating ground, apparently never quite grasping the concept that the group is relevant only as it enables members to live richer lives *outside* the weekly interaction experience.

No great harm is done by this fixated behavior until the professional group member decides to apply his learnings as a leader. He naively assumes that his high degree of expertise as member qualifies him to be responsible for the membership of others. He repeats the error once made by the profession as a whole—that the skills needed to function as group member are interchangeable with the skills needed to function as group leader.

The group leader who is a misuser of groups often is the one who uses the Personal-Assertive (HIM, Cell II C, Hill, 1965) behavior against members to start group interaction; for example, he is likely to say, "You turn me off," "I don't believe you," "That is a bunch

188

of garbage," or "You keep looking at John in a hostile manner; tell him what you dislike about him," etc., ad nauseam. The incompetent ex-group-member-turned-leader terms this hostile interchange "confrontation" and feels that the group was productive if members learned to attack one another. He sees the name of the game as "Seek out, destroy, enjoy." For these misusers, to experience group as a warm, sustaining process is unknown; to experience confrontation as an act of grace is incomprehensible; and to suggest that the group need not be negative is inconceivable.

Groups have come under severe attack, and the experiences of groups led by irresponsible, incompetent "leaders" have made many of these attacks justified. Gary Allen's (1968) classic masterpiece of propaganda, "Hate Therapy," published by the American Opinion Press is basically an attack on irresponsible group leadership. When Allen characterizes all groups as a devious Communist plot to undermine the United States, he leaves something to be desired in accurate reporting, but his stance that some groups *do* harm people is certainly accurate. On this one point the authors of this book are in complete accord with Allen's position, but they feel it would be tragic if all groups were avoided because some are harmful. It would seem a responsibility of the profession to adopt a set of minimal training standards necessary to qualify group leaders and to issue a Certification of Competency to those who do qualify.

HOW TO AVOID A TOXIC GROUP

The fact that groups can be misused suggests that the responsible group leader should be prepared to supply prospective members with guidelines which will provide them with direction in selecting a group. Shostrom (1970:150) offers a list of seven ways to avoid groups which may be, in his words, "stupid, dangerous, corrupt, and even fatal."

STRICT NOs!

1. Never answer newspaper ads for group experience, as it is forbidden ethically to advertise.

2. Never participate in groups with less than six members or more than sixteen, as scapegoating and ganging-up can occur.

189

3. Never join on an impulse, and if you find yourself in a group where everyone talks group jargon, walk out.

4. Never participate in a group encounter with close associates.

5. Never be impressed by beautiful or class-signaled surroundings as good groups can occur anywhere.

6. Never stay with a group which has a behavioral axe to grind, e.g., cultural, sexual, intellectual, etc.

7. Never participate in a group whose leader lacks formal connection with a profession on which you can check.

These guidelines can serve only as a gross selector. The best insurance is for a prospective group member to read the literature on groups so that he has a realistic perception of what to expect from the experience and will have the confidence to leave a group if he makes an unfortunate choice.

The authors of this volume feel that a nourishing group will be characterized by these dynamics:

1. Each member will come prepared to work. This attitude is crystallized in the individual pre-group session.

2. The group will be into meaningful interaction very soon.

3. Laughter will be as frequent as tears.

4. The leader will be active but not dominant. He will be in touch with all members all the time.

5. Members and leaders will look forward to the group sessions most of the time and will leave with a sense of having been nourished.

6. "Acting out" behaviors will be little evidenced.

7. Members will risk themselves more and more as they come to care more for one another.

COMMERCIAL MATERIALS

The proliferation of "parlor games" exploiting the popularity of what may be the growth vehicle of our century—the group experience —attests to the alertness of entrepreneurs, but this proliferation also attests to the urgency of the profession's advancing a position statement concerning groups and standards of training for group leaders. An examination of current materials offered for sale is at once distressing and intriguing.

Leaderless Group Tapes

Commercially prepared "Encounter Tapes" are being sold, some to professionals and some to the general public. The tapes consist of a series of taped instruction designed to lead participants through an "encounter" group without a leader. The instruction includes goals and some basic rules; the group structure is then developed through a series of exercises. Between exercises, time is allowed for discussion of individual behaviors and reactions of participants. The programs include micro-labs, strength bombardment, feedback, and non-verbal exercises.

The tapes were originally developed under the guise of meeting the urgent need for trained leaders. The first tapes were training exercises to prepare non-professional (students, housewives, patients, *etc.*) to function as group leaders. Shostrom (1970) indicates that perhaps this trend grows out of the attempt to discard the doctor-patient model and view the group leader as one of the "guys."

The use of leaderless group tapes has become almost a fad. In their creation apparently little thought was given to what happens when the tape recorder is turned off or the party breaks up or couples go home. To achieve a successful group experience, apparently all that is needed is the series of tapes, a tape player, space, and willing participants. One member places the tape on the machine, turns it on, and they all follow the recorded directions.

Stoller (1970), in his critique of encounter tapes, titled the article "Painless Deflowering of the Group Virgin." The tapes offer *instruction* only, and missing is the modeling, facilitating, traffic directing, and interaction stimulation which a group leader supplies. Group membership is a learned phenomenon and, though the taped instructions are stated clearly, there is no built-in safeguard that a given group will have a positive, growth-producing experience. The tapes

191

do create a desire to know more about the group process, but do not make clear the uniqueness of group experiences. While the writers of this book are in sympathy with the acute need for trained group leaders, we cannot accept the proposal that a tape recorder can serve as a "reasonable facsimile" of a competent, responsible group leader. We also recognize, however, that encounter tapes are consonant with the phenomenological position concerning the nature of man. (See discussion in Appendix A, Historical Foundations.)

Group Games

There are a number of commercially-prepared "group games" available to the general public which can be purchased in department stores, stationery stores, and in some toy stores. These have intriguing titles, e.g., "Group Therapy," "Seduction," and "Bundling." All are designed as parlor games for "adults" who may be interested in dabbling in the "psychological arts." All exploit the group process. The following descriptions, which are the manufacturers' advertisements, give a flavor of what might be expected:

GROUP THERAPY. The game asks people to perform various verbal or physical tasks. It's a guide, an excuse, and a structure for frank communication among people. $8.50.

SENSITIVITY. A game of psychodrama, or role-playing, designed to help an individual learn more about himself and how he identifies with other people. $10.00.

INSIGHT. Each player makes his appraisal of the personality of each other player and himself. An informal fun game for stimulating conversation. $8.50.

GAMES PEOPLE PLAY. Based on Dr. Eric Berne's best selling book on the psychology of human relationships. Three game boards. $10.00.

SEDUCTION. Matches two couples in a witty game of strategy. Each "lover" pursues and attempts to "seduce" one member of the opposite sex while avoiding seduction by another. $6.50.

BUNDLING. Now an adult game. Was an old custom and a

form of "night-wooing" where two people lying side by side, fully clothed, and covered with a single blanket were separated by a bundling board. Now the science of psychology has coupled with the art of "bundling" and the results are a most intriguing Psycho-Sensual experience. $6.50.

MISUSE OF GROUPS IN PUBLIC SCHOOLS

The commercial exploitation of groups is motivated clearly by profit needs. The misuse of groups by ex-professional-grouper-turned-leader is more obscurely motivated by neurotic needs. The misuse of groups in public institutions is motivated by good intentions, but these good intentions often stem from a misperception of the realities of limitations imposed on groups which deal with minors who are in required attendance. Group counseling with students, even though self-referred, demands a restricted set of parameters which are not necessary in adult groups. Counselors in public institutions have a clear responsibility to the parents of students and to the institution as well as the counselees. Such responsibilities impose boundaries for the group counselor which should be understood clearly both by the leader and by the members of the group. These responsibilities have been discussed thoroughly in previous chapters.

The literature is abundant with uses of group processes for like student problems, including discipline, underachievement, absenteeism, *etc.* The position of the writers that group counseling goals *per se* are not appropriate on a group basis has been made clear in previous chapters. Group counseling membership is an individuation process for individual growth need; thus each group counseling member should be self-referred and should, in conjunction with the group leader, develop individually-stated objectives. Groups based on commonalities such as underachievement, discipline, or attendance problems are guidance groups and are primarily aimed at enculturation; these groups have a group goal. At times counselors have used a group guidance format to "seduce" members into becoming a counseling group. This is unethical.

Another misuse of public school group counseling is the marathon technique of keeping students out of classes for long periods of time, or the weekend method where groups are held off-campus, usually at a resort. It is not the writers' position to argue for or against the effectiveness of the marathon approach, but only to state that marathon techniques are not appropriate for counselors working with student groups in the public school setting.

At times public school counselors are tempted to use students as co-leaders. This seems to be an exploitation of the student which cannot be justified on the rationale of lack of a sufficient number of professionally trained staff to serve as group leaders. That older students may be used as resource persons in guidance groups such as freshman orientation, part-time employment, or narcotics is acceptable, and at times appropriate; however, to use students as co-counselors in group counseling is *not* appropriate.

A final comment regarding the misuse of groups in a public institutional setting concerns confidentiality. A counselor cannot assume that student counseling groups will maintain confidentiality; in fact, the opposite will probably be the case. If the counselor works from the Extensional group model, this is no problem, as focus is on the here-and-now rather than the there-and-then In any theoretical paradigm, however, the counselor cannot guarantee that content of the group process will not go beyond the group, certainly not through the leader but perhaps through some of the members. Thus for a group counselor to assume that groups of students can keep the level of confidentiality that adult groups can maintain is naive and irresponsible, and leads to a serious misuse of groups. The group counselor can only guarantee to the group that *he* will keep content confidential; he cannot make this guarantee for members. At times there is pressure on group leaders to report to the administration the material discussed in a counseling group. The counselor's ethical code gives direction in this dilemma—the conflict between his responsibility to the students and his responsibility to the institution. Ethics require that a counselor report a *condition* which might be harmful to students; he does not report a student. When it is necessary that a counselor report a condition (i.e., sale of marijuana, availablity of alcohol) he of course informs the group that he is doing so.

SUMMARY

The above comments have suggested that the group leader be as aware as possible of his own human needs. Shepard's (1970, p. 11) words are worth remembering, ". . . it is beneficial for both patients and therapists to be reminded that those in charge of directing, molding, and healing the human psyche are themselves human and therefore fallible."

The world of group provides an experience unique in our culture, an experience which is designed to enable participants to lead more fulfilled lives. But when those unique experiences appropriate in group are transmitted inappropriately outside group, travesties can result. Herein lies a source of misuse of groups, and it is particularly apparent in the commercial exploitation of what is a delicate, fragile process.

The delicacy of the process as well as its infinite intricacy also has implications for group leadership. This chapter has been emphatic that group membership does *not* prepare a member to lead a group. The violation of this truism presents a serious professional concern.

BIBLIOGRAPHY

Allen, Gary. "Hate Therapy—Sensitivity Training for Planned Change," *American Opinion,* Jan. 1968.

Hill, Wm. Fawcett. *Hill Interaction Matrix.* Los Angeles: Youth Studies Center, University of Southern California, 1965.

Howard, Jane. *Please Touch.* New York: McGraw-Hill, 1970.

Mentz, Alexander. "Non-Adaptive Group Behavior." *The Journal of Abnormal and Social Psychology,* Vol. 46, April, 1951, pp. 150-59.

Shepard, Martin, and Lee, Marjorie. *Games Analysts Play.* New York: G. P. Putnam Sons, 1970.

Shostrom, Everett L. "Group Therapy: Let the Buyer Beware." *Readings in Psychology Today.* CRM Books, Del Mar, Ca., 1970, pp. 149-51.

Stoller, Frederick H. "Encounter Tapes," *Psychology Today,* Sept. 1970, pp. 18-22.

CHAPTER 14

THE ARTS OF GROUPSMANSHIP

- The Fine Art of Handling a Groupsman's Groupsmanship
- The Fine Art of Groupsmanship or Surviving in Group Interaction
- A Sequel to the Fine Art of Groupsmanship: The Advanced Art of Groupsmanship
- Ready Reference Finder for the Groupsman

To the Group Leader:

May you never have as a group member the groups-man we have satirized in this chapter! We hope, however, that our tongue-in-cheek presentation will alert you to behaviors which do not facilitate productive group interaction.

CHAPTER 14

THE ARTS OF GROUPSMANSHIP

In this chapter we will present two satires caricaturizing various behaviors we have observed in group interaction which obstruct the process. First "The Fine Art of Groupsmanship" is presented, followed by "The Advanced Art of Groupsmanship." A "Ready Reference Guide for the Groupsman" completes the chapter. The following brief comments address Groupsmanship from the viewpoint of the group leader and states what he can do about the behaviors of a groupsman.

THE FINE ART OF HANDLING A GROUPSMAN'S GROUPSMANSHIP

The art of handling a groupsman rests mainly in identifying his gambits and recognizing when there is one in the group. Once the leaders know the techniques of these professional obstructors of positive group interaction, they can usually handle any of the ploys.

The mistakes a beginning leader might make in working with a groupsman may involve finding himself, the leader, interacting at the level on which a groupsman operates. If, however, the leader studies carefully the chapters on the roles and functions of group leadership, he will have the necessary techniques for dealing with groupsmanship antics. The concept that each of us is essentially talking about ourself should be reinforced if a member is exhibiting the types of behaviors leaders recognize as groupsmanship.

It is important that leaders realize that most groupsmen do *not* deliberately practice these gambits for the purpose of disrupting interaction. Usually the groupsman is sincere, but unaware of appropriate and helpful mores of group behavior. Seldom is a groupsman aware of what he is doing. Our two satires are presented in a humorous vein for the purpose of making leaders and members conscious of maneuvers which do not belong in group interaction; we are not suggesting that such a creature as the groupsman described actually exists (we hope!) .

THE FINE ART OF GROUPSMANSHIP
OR
SURVIVING IN GROUP INTERACTION[1]

The counselor who is not trained in group process is a counselor only half-trained. The counselor who cannot make references to "when I was leading my group the other day . . ." is not keeping up with professional trends. The modern counselor without a group is like a Rogerian without an "ummm. . . ," which is all well and good. As a profession we are expanding our talents into an area where they will be more visible than they were in the sanctity of the individual counseling session. True, we could always produce tape recordings, but somehow this was never quite as satisfactory as having a live audience. So I consider the current movement to groupness to be a good thing for our collective ego strength as a profession. We will be glad we did it, unless. . . .

And it is to this "unless" that I wish to address these remarks. I would like to call attention to some of the hazards inherent in the group movement of which counselors, who are notoriously innocent, may not be fully aware. Since I consider counselors by definition my friends, I feel it is my professional duty to apprise them of these pitfalls before it is too late. And when it is too late is when they unwittingly, naively, and defenselessly find themselves a group *member,* rather than a group *leader.* Now obviously the most intelligent move for any counselor to make is to avoid becoming a member of a group. You walk away when a "friend" suggests that to be the very best group leader you must of course have experience as a group member and, since this is so, and, since he just happened to know where a group was meeting, why don't you join, and you do, and before you can emit another "umm" there you are sitting in a circle, unwitting,

---

1. Originally published by Marilyn Bates as "The Fine Art of Groupsmanship." *Personnel and Guidance Journal,* Dec. 1968, Vol. 47, #4, pp. 381-384.

naive, and defenseless. So since you weren't smart enough to insist that "once a group leader always a group leader," salvaging the situation best you can is all that's left for you to do. Unfortunately, this requires learning yet another skill, one which was *not* taught to you in your formal training. In the trade this skill is known as the Fine Art of Groupsmanship or Surviving in Group Interaction. You must understand that when you begin practicing Groupsmanship you are practicing an art which is not to be broadcast to the profession in general. You must abide by the ethical standards of Groupsmanship which require that only selected initiates be instructed in the Art. Because if everyone knew the ploys, where would that leave us? You are right: unwitting, naive, and defenseless!

Now that the confidentiality of these remarks is fully understood, let us get on with it. You will, of course, be developing ploys and gambits of upsmanship on your own as time goes by, but these basic maneuvers which I am going to outline should get you through these first dangerous group meetings where you have so unwittingly, naively, and defenselessly allowed yourself to be a member. First of all, remember that surviving in the group process arena demands the most aggressive form of Groupsmanship. The main, essential, cardinal, Number One Rule is: ATTACK BEFORE YOU ARE AT-TACKED! Never, under any circumstances, sit back passively and await developments. This is sheer suicide. If you do this, it is only a matter of time, and an incredibly short time at that, before the group turns on you, fangs bared and claws unsheathed, snarling into your innermost privacy, aided and abetted in this maneuver by the group leader, who knows full well which side *his* bread is buttered on! And the only way to defend yourself against mass group attack is to attack, promiscuously and indiscriminately. Ideally, in order to exhibit the finest degree of skill, you should intuit the sensitive spots of your opponents around the circle and level your probes in those directions, but at the outset you cannot, for the sake of survival, insist on holding up the finer standards of Groupsmanship. The best initial procedure is to fire volleys broadside into the group, couching your comments on a personal level, preferably using some other group as reference. For example, you might begin by saying, "I have never been a member of a group which had such trouble getting started." This remark immediately places the members on the defensive, having

201

been tried and found wanting, and has the added virtue of happening to be true—you never have been a group member before.

Now it is vital that neophyte Groupsmen realize the importance of phrasing comments in terms against which other members have no defense. For example, an excellent ploy is to express in loud, authoritative tones, preferably preceded by a vigorous sigh, and prefaced by some preliminary shifting about in your chair: "This group bores me! I can hardly keep from yawning in your faces. You are all such phonies, talking on and on and never really saying anything." Examine the power of that attack for a moment and its Groupsmanship will be immediately evident. First of all, you have attacked with an unprovable statement—the group is boring—and have subtly placed the onus for this state of affairs on group members. They cannot demonstrate that the group isn't boring—you just proved that it was by stating so in a loud comment. And since they *are* the group, it follows that as individuals they are boring. And so each is exquisitely pinned, helpless to respond, feeling guilty at having given you so much discomfort in having to suppress your yawns. Also, calling them all "phonies" is most effective, since neither you nor they know what *that* means, except that is the WORST POSSIBLE THING TO BE as a group member. So immediately you have the situation entirely in hand.

But don't rest now! You have just begun to practice Groupsmanship. You must continue to press your advantage. One way to do this is to grasp at a member's remark—almost any remark will do—and intently ask, "*Why* did you do that . . ." or "*Why* did you say that. . ." whichever is appropriate. Now since "why" is an unanswerable question, you have manipulated a group member into a corner from which he will have to struggle for some time to extricate himself, during which time you are perfectly safe from attack. But a warning: You may be so diverted by the spectacle of your victim struggling to deal with what you know full well is an impossible question you may be tempted to rest your attack. DON'T.

Although the question "why" is an unparalleled tool of Groupsmanship, actually any question, AS LONG AS IT FOCUSES ON OTHERS AND NOT ON YOU, is excellent for defense. You can say, wisely looking up at the ceiling, with a distant look in your eye, cheeks sucked in, "Don't you think that means you really hate your mother?" or, also very good, "You really don't understand yourself very well, do you?" A third choice of great power is to accuse a member of having a "hang-up" about something or other. This makes an excellent *coup de grace* and skilled Groupsmen like to use it for the kill, but as a beginner feel free to use any of these ploys at will. They all set you up as possessing superior psychological wisdom and, if you continually attack, you can keep the group so far off balance that they are never able to see through your Groupsmanship.

If by an unfortunate chance there is another Groupsman aboard, you might run into a little trouble, but there is a surefire ploy with which you can defend your position successfully. It is more than likely that the other Groupsman will turn and question you. The thing to do *immediately and firmly* is to turn the question back onto him. For example, he, pressing *his attack*, ruminates somberly, leveling his comment toward you: "I wonder why you made that remark?" Your instant retort without a flicker of hesitation (and timing is most important to the Groupsman) is to counter with, "Something about me bothers you?" Now the skill with which this gambit is parried depends on the experience of your Groupsman opponent, but you can keep turning the question back onto him indefinitely. Also, some uninitiated group member, impatient with this apparently aimless interchange, will eventually intervene and then you can both, with the elegant grace of a fencing team, drive your rapiers into this helpless member. He will never know what happened. But if for an instant you let your guard down and are inclined to feel even a moment of remorse, remember *you* could be the next victim. So keep attacking at all costs. Pity is a luxury a Groupsman cannot afford!

Another excellent gambit in Groupsmanship is to give advice—particularly unasked-for advice. Nothing is more irritating to other members than this tactic, and by keeping them in a constant state of annoyance you will keep them vulnerable to your attacks. Frequent judgmental use of "I think you should . . ." or "You ought to have done thus and so . . ." is most effective. And if you can word your advice so that a member should have behaved differently in the *past,* you are functioning at high level Groupsmanship. Suggesting changes in past behavior is considered top form since it represents an impossibility, yet does it so subtly that the recipient is left helpless to cope with the advice and, hence, with you.

Group Leadership

Groupsmanship can also be practiced by keeping conversation focused on topics rather than on group members. A skilled Groupsman can keep a group discussing the weather, or last night's ball game, or principles of mental hygiene for endless sessions. A variation of this ploy is for you to keep talking endlessly on a meaningless (impersonal) topic. This is good Groupsmanship because, remember, when members are discussing these irrelevant topics, they are *not* discussing YOU, which, as you well know by now, is to be avoided. Of course, probably nothing is happening in the group which is of value and lots of time is being wasted, but suppress such thoughts as those immediately! A secondary rule of Groupsmanship which must be remembered: *A Groupsman does not worry about wasting a group's time.* His only motive is to survive any way that he can.

The most dangerous opponent a Groupsman encounters will be the group leader, but there are known Upsmanships developed to deal with this problem effectively. (Incidentally, the greatest score a Groupsman can record is to force the group leader to walk out of a group even temporarily. While this is not likely to happen to a beginning Groupsman, still, ethics of the Corps require that all such successes be reported in the professional journals immediately!) But let us attend to maneuvers of Groupsmen *vs.* leader. The particular ploys to be exercised against the leader depend to some extent on the style of group leading which is being exhibited. If the leader used the "You feel . . ." or "I hear you saying . . ." he can be disposed of rather easily. Just use the turn-the-comment-back-onto-him methodology illustrated earlier and he is helpless. Or, even if his comments are absolutely accurate, deny them, implying by your tone of voice "What a stupid remark!" It will not be long before you will find yourself ignored by this type of leader. Which leaves you completely free to attack.

Now, if the leader happens to work in the much more dangerous (to you) style of confrontation, your defense should be somewhat different. Beware of the leader who insists on being honest, open, and authentic. Try to avoid such a group if you can. Leave such a group as soon as possible, if by some unfortunate error you have not *avoided it.* But until you can make good your escape, there are a few, albeit weak, Groupsmanship gambits which you can employ as temporary protection. One is to respond to a confrontation made by the leader to you with a blank, uncomprehending stare. Look confused, refuse to hear what he said, and make a response which in no way reflects any understanding on your part. For instance, suppose he risks himself with the remark, "I think you are copping out and this makes me angry with you." The Groupsman should look puzzled, furrow his brow, and ask innocently, "Could you explain what cop-out means?" The leader probably will be so frustrated that for the rest of the evening he will ignore you, which is good, for remember, what you are after is survival. As stated above, the only sensible course of action when dealing with the leader who insists on working at confrontation is to get out of the group altogether, pleading a sick aunt or something. But there are other ways of handling the honest efforts of such a leader until you can escape. One is to avoid looking directly at him. Rather, in response to his remarks, throw up your hands, shrug your shoulders helplessly, turn to the group, and say, "I wonder why our leader finds it necessary to pick on me. . . ." This immediately focuses the spotlight on the leader. If he refuses the bait, he is ducking the issue. If he responds, he admits guilt. Either way he is hooked and for the time being helpless—which is what you want. A general rule of thumb when dealing with the leader who works at confrontation is: when working with an authentic leader, the good Groupsman will meet honesty with dishonesty. A sub-rule: Avoid eye contact. A sub-sub-rule: Get out as soon as possible. The honor of Groupsmanship is at stake.

Now that the beginning Groupsman has become more skilled in this Art, it is time to turn attention to some of the finer points of Groupsmanship. These should not be attempted by the neophyte until he has mastered thoroughly all the preceding gambits, as the following ploys require fine control and finesse and are not likely to be effective if the Groupsman has erred in any way and allowed himself to come under attack.

One most useful upsmanship which can be used to divert even the most sophisticated group is for the Groupsman to bring up, *in great detail,* some involved problem concerning his wife, or his mother-in-law, or his teen-ager. This ploy gives the appearance of the Groupsman talking about his personal problems while actually he is scapegoating a member of his family. More than likely the group will enjoy dissecting, and analyzing, and the Groupsman can counter with a game of "Yes, but. . . ." The more lurid the tale (it need not be true, you understand), the more effective the transaction. Seldom does even the leader realize that the Groupsman is using someone outside the group to keep attention away from himself, thereby in a subtle way following his primary rule—avoid attack.

Another way to practice refined Groupsmanship is to arrange an expression on your face which transmits that you are listening intently. Lean slightly forward in your chair and focus concentratedly on whoever is speaking. *Then tune out completely.* You will soon get the reputation of being an excellent listener without ever having to become involved with the group. Because, however, at any moment you may be asked for a response, Groupsmanship requires that you select a notion expressed by a member just before you tune out, and be prepared on a moment's notice to explain that you were intently examining the ramifications of that previous remark; it had such *great* significance. *And you quote the remark verbatim.* This is known as the fine art of having-your-cake-and-eating-it-too in Groupsmanship parlance.

The practiced Groupsman has an extensive repertoire of psychological constructs which he can "name drop." This subtle form of attack requires a knowledge of several models of the group process. Then, if the attack is pressing in, the Groupsman can (1) lapse into parent-adult-child jargon, à la Berne's (1964) games model; or he can (2) pontifically point out that such and such a behavior represented "Gate-keeping" in Bales' (1955) model; or (3) categorize the areas in *Hill's Interaction Matrix* (1965). If necessary, of course, the Groupsman can always invent a model on the spot, but this is not considered sporting and should only be done in a crisis. Better to have two or three legitimate conceptual schemes ready to name-drop in self-defense, the best form of which, as any Groupsman knows, is attack.

It is to be hoped that by now the unwitting, naive, and defenseless beginner is a practiced Groupsman, having studied these directions carefully. Groupsmanship is a fine art practiced by only a noble few, who have the courage and finesse to avoid group interaction. But the reward is great. As Groupsman you will survive all group sessions unchanged, untouched, uninvolved—an un-person.

BIBLIOGRAPHY

Bales, Robert F. "How People Interact in Conferences." *Scientific American Reprint,* March 1955.

Bates, Marilyn. "The Fine Art of Groupsmanship." *Personnel and Guidance Journal,* Dec. 1968, Vol. 47, #4, pp. 381-384.

Berne, Eric. *Games People Play.* New York: Grove Press, 1964.

Hill, Wm. Fawcett. *Hill Interaction Matrix.* Los Angeles: Youth Study Center, University of Southern California, 1965.

A SEQUEL TO THE FINE ART OF GROUPSMANSHIP: THE ADVANCED ART OF GROUPSMANSHIP

I am glad to report that, since the introduction of Groupsmanship as a fine art to the profession some years ago (Bates, 1968), the practice has been spreading. I have personally witnessed an exceptional display several times during the past months, and I am sure you have been similarly inspired. In case you need to review any of the basic ploys I have included the original article, "The Fine Art of Groupsmanship," preceding these comments, but I am confident that by now you have the elementary procedures well in hand and are ready to advance your art to a more refined level. I must again remind you, however, of the extreme confidentiality of my remarks. We who practice Groupsmanship simply cannot afford to be promiscuous with a careless broadcast of the techniques, for, as you well know, some of the power of this noble art is based on the hidden agenda of Groupsmanship—surviving group interaction without getting involved. All of us Groupsmen are dedicated to the proposition of maintaining our *status quo* as un-persons who will go to any length to avoid personal growth.

As you also know by now, it is customary to recognize by a moment of silence our illustrious and worthy founding father, Stephen Potter (n.d.), who blessed us with his fine comments concerning Lifesmanship, Upsmanship, and Gamesmanship. We Groupsmen follow in the tradition of a great man who taught us so well how to win at the game of life while enjoying the pleasures of Upsmanship, i.e., the theory and practice of putting people down without their being aware of it.

We also owe much to Phillip Broughton (n.d.), who contributed

Wordsmanship to our repertoire. You will recall that Phil hit upon a sure-fire method for converting report-writing frustration into a delightful exercise in hacking through etymological thickets. In case you have lost your notes I will reprint Broughton's lexicon of thirty carefully chosen words:

Column 1	*Column 2*	*Column 3*
0. integrated	0. management	0. options
1. total	1. organizational	1. flexibility
2. systematized	2. monitored	2. capability
3. parallel	3. reciprocal	3. mobility
4. functional	4. digital	4. programming
5. responsive	5. logistical	5. concept
6. optional	6. transitional	6. time-phase
7. synchronized	7. incremental	7. projection
8. compatible	8. third-generation	8. hardware
9. balanced	9. policy	9. contingency

The procedure is simple. Think of any three-digit number, then select the corresponding buzzword from each column. For example, number 257 produces "systematized logistical projection," a phrase which can be dropped into virtually any report with that ring of decisive, knowledgeable authority. Wordsmanship is guaranteed to impress people with our skills in report-writing by this systematic method of combining meaningless words. "No one will have the remotest idea of what you're talking about," says Broughton, "but the important thing is they are not about to admit it."

These two great artists, Potter and Broughton, provide impressive models of courage and finesse. As we negotiate the dangerous shoals of the group process, we can gain courage from their fortitude and wisdom. I am sure that by now you have mastered the more basic points of Groupsmanship and know well the cardinal rule: AT-TACK BEFORE YOU ARE ATTACKED. I am sure also that you have thoroughly stilled any qualms you might have had about wasting group time and are abiding carefully by the sub-rule of meeting honesty with dishonesty. I hope that you have avoided confrontations successfully and have ceaselessly pressed questions on other group members, particularly probing with whys, and freely sprinkling shoulds and oughts about.

Now you are ready to refine your techniques. I must warn you that these advanced ploys are somewhat harder to maneuver without bringing yourself under attack, but with concentration you should be able to master them fairly rapidly.

First of all, you must immediately purchase *Bruiser's Dictionary of Four-Letter Pornographic Words From Twenty Languages.* This is a rich resource of colorful phrases which are essential for the advanced Groupsman to have at his tongue's tip. Group members will be most impressed by your ability to move to "gut-level" fast. After all, if you are expressing yourself in colorful, unmentionable four-letter words, you *must* be expressing real feelings. You may use English if you will, but it is much better to drop these succulent phrases in a foreign language—preferably switching from one language to another—the more the better. Begin with Italian since it sounds the most earthy. You understand, of course, that it is not necessary to recall all the meanings, or for that matter, even know them; just drop them generously into group interaction as frequently as possible and you will immediately establish your superior skill at getting down to basic, gut-level interaction.

Another Advanced Groupsmanship technique involves nonverbal interaction. The idea here is to suggest some nonverbal exercise such as back-rubbing (or front-rubbing if you dare) , or gazing intently into someone's eyes for a long period of time, or milling about with your eyes closed for five minutes or so, or feeling about someone's face, beard, and all—anything will do, really. You, groupsman, will suggest these exercises for the sake of the exercise. You will have no purpose in mind; you will just suggest playing games with nonverbal communication for the sake of passing time with game-playing. The Group will be impressed with these clever little sports and each member will think *he* is the only one who does not know the purpose of the exercise, so will be afraid to expose his stupidity by asking. Thus, you can enjoy the session, having avoided meaningful interaction entirely.

An extremely effective Groupsman ploy is for you to probe into the personal lives of other members by asking pointed questions. For example, ask another member about his sex life or how often he masturbates. Most group members will hesitate or refuse to answer because then they would be accused of holding back and not being a

Good Group Member. They will stumble about, embarrassed and hating every minute of it, but will haltingly try to answer. Little do they know that they are in the hands of a Master of the Art of Groupsmanship and are being had—their privacy invaded in the name of the group process. Little do they know that all they have to do is to refuse to answer the questions by saying, "I don't wish to talk about that" and stand on it. Instead they try, and try, and try, getting in deeper and deeper, while you, the happy Groupsman, enjoy the spectacle.

Another ploy you might practice is built around the notion that somewhere inside of each of us we have a peculiar homunculus, a sort of little man who represents our *REAL SELF* buried deep within. You can capitalize on this peculiar idea and turn it to your advantage. The trick employed is to gaze intently into someone's eyes and plead, "I really would like to get to know the REAL YOU. I want to know who you *really* are." This leaves the poor recipient of this technique quite helpless. He has been forced into a position of somehow having to dredge up a mysterious creature from inside himself and trot it out as "THE REAL ME." Now since he has no way at all of producing this creature, he is at a total loss and can only mutter, "But, but this *is* me—this is what I am . . ." which is never enough for us Groupsmen who practice the fine art of keeping others off balance, avoiding meaningful interaction. You can put down your victim even further by turning to the group with a knowing look and an expressive shrug of your shoulders and disgusted shake of your head. The member who could not produce his REAL ME can only cower mutely, branded with the label "Uncooperative Cop-out."

A very simply ploy, but one which is 100% effective in completely stopping group interaction, is for a Groupsman to ask someone to define a word. Nothing is more annoying and nothing stops communication quite so quickly. For example, an authentic, honest member may be trying to communicate his feelings of friendship toward another member of the group. The Groupsman can successfully intervene and prevent interaction by assertively asking for a definition of friendship. "What do you mean by friendship? I think you had better define it before we go on. You might not both be meaning the same thing." Thus, the interchange is brought up to the

210

conventional level and feelings left hopelessly behind, beautifully and skillfully.

An advanced Groupsman is quite adept at Super-mothering. I am sure you have seen this manipulation in action many times and may even have done some s'mothering yourself. It goes like this. Suppose someone is trying to deal with an area which concerns him—his feelings of being put down every time another group member speaks, for example. As Groupsman, you quickly move in and "protect" the person who is being confronted, putting words in his mouth, making "helpful" comments such as, "I'm sure he really doesn't *mean* to offend you," or "He didn't sound like that to me." Anything which will prevent the two members from honestly dealing with their relationship will satisfy a Groupsman, who gains doubly from this ploy. Besides blocking honest confrontation, you appear to the group as a Knight-in-Shining-Armor, a latter-day Florence Nightingale, who is bravely rescuing another member from distress. The fact that you are practicing Advanced Groupsmanship in the form of Super-mothering goes unnoticed by the group

Another excellent ploy which a Groupsman can use is to talk *about* another member, rather than confront him face to face. You and another member can "gossip" about him in the group at length, never asking what the member concerned thinks or feels. You never allow him the opportunity to speak for himself. This ploy avoids honest confrontation and allows members to speculate endlessly about the motives, personalities, feelings, etc., etc., of others in the group. Since the person directly concerned is never addressed directly, the game can go on and on, preserving the main rule of Groupsmanship —Surviving group interaction, completely uninvolved.

There are several Groupsmanship gambits particularly suited to the Groupsman leader. You, as Groupsman leader, if you are skilled, can get double mileage from the fee collected for running the group. You do this by using your groups for your own needs. Thus, if you have had a fight with your wife, you can charge into group and emote all over the place, happily discharging your pent-up hostilities on the group members and *getting paid in the process!* This is known in Groupsmanship parlance as *Having Your Cake and Eating It Too.*

Another fun thing for a Groupsman leader is to create a "Hot Seat" arrangement. It goes like this. Someone is in the "it" seat and you, as Groupsman leader, probe and fire questions and analyze this "it" with a great deal of authoritative hostility. You come on as a knowledgeable expert who has all the answers and thus can meet your ego needs very nicely, while also enjoying the pleasures of airing your hostilities. There is not likely to be much interference from group members, because they don't want to be next on the hot seat and be It, so they keep their mouths firmly shut, allowing you to enjoy yourself and control the group with an iron hand.

The M & M technique is an excellent Groupsman ploy for the leader to polish up. In this procedure you carefully reinforce comments, behaviors, attitudes which you, group leader, find palatable. For example, if you like members to express themselves in four letter words, you M & M this with nods, smiles, and approval. If you happen to have a need for psychological voyeurism, you happily reinforce members to relate in minute detail stories of their personal, private lives. Using the M & M technique you can send the content of group discussion in any direction you choose to meet your own needs and shape the behaviors of members in directions which you, group leader, approve—which, most likely, will be a carbon copy of yourself.

A couple of minor points—the Groupsman leader, or member, for that matter, can constantly chime in with frequent "I don't believe you's." Whenever a member seems to be getting someplace, interject a "I don't believe you" in a firm, loud, authoritative tone of voice, and interaction is stopped cold. Also, frequent use of UMMMmmm's and constant parroting of "You feel" or maximum use of silence which is without meaning will preserve the goals of no interaction in the group.

One of the more subtle points of Groupsmanship on the part of the leader involves maneuvering members into being treated like objects. One fine way to do this is to ask a member to pretend some part of his body does not belong to him and to carry on a conversation with that part. For example, a member might be asked to talk to his hands or to his feet, or to a chair which represents some part of himself. This is an effective way to avoid person-to-person interaction while causing the group member to experience himself as object rather than subject. This is usually done in the name of the here-and-now, but comes on *it* and *me* rather than *I* and *Thou*. As long as the victim is not allowed to experience himself as one whole, he will have difficulty interacting with other members of the group—and thus will avoid encounter, which is always the hidden agenda of Groupsmanship, whether practiced by leader or by member.

A final word concerning the professional grouper—that practiced Groupsman who again might be either leader or member, but who uses the group process as an end in itself. He will ride the group circuit—Kairos to Topanga Canyon to Esalen to Kairos, round and round and round—never changing, always wallowing in the acting-out process often seen as group interaction *par excellence,* refining his Groupsmanship techniques, enjoying his skills, and most especially, enjoying the discomforts of his victims. Groupsmanship can become almost a way of life. The primary purpose of using the group process—to extend positive life space—gets lost from sight. This can happen to anyone, but most especially it can happen to those who practice: The Advanced Art of Groupsmanship.

Bibliography

Bates, Marilyn. "The Fine Art of Groupsmanship." *Personnel and Guidance Journal,* Dec., 1968, Vol. 47, No. 4, pp. 381-384.

Broughton, Phillip. "How to Win at Wordsmanship," unpublished mimeographed paper, U.S. Public Health Service, no date.

Potter, Stephen. *The Theory and Practice of Gamesmanship or the Art of Winning Games Without Actually Cheating.* New York: Holt, Rinehart and Winston, No year.

Note: For the convenience of the reader who wishes to polish his Groupsmanship, the following Ready Reference Guide is given here.

READY REFERENCE FINDER FOR THE GROUPSMAN

1. Attack before you are attacked.
   "I have never been in a group which had so much trouble getting started."
2. Turn about on a member's remark.
   "Why did you say that?"
3. Ask questions which focus on others.
   "Don't you think what you said means that you hate your mother?"

"You really don't understand yourself very well, do you?"

"You really have a hang-up about that, don't you?"

4. Against the "attack" of another groupsman, ploy with "Something about me bothers you?"

5. Give unasked-for advice.

"I think you should (have done) . . . or ought to have done . . ."

6. Keep conversation focused on topics, not group members. (Never worry about wasting the group's time.)

7. In dealing with the leader who works at confrontation, meet honesty with dishonesty and manipulation.

"I wonder why our leader finds it necessary to pick on me?"

"I don't understand what you mean by cop-out. Would you define it?".

8. Relate an involved problem concerning someone other than yourself such as your wife, mother-in-law, etc.

9. Arrange an expression on your face which reflects intent listening, then tune out. Remember the last comment made by a group member.

10. "Name drop" psychological terms (especially to members unfamiliar with them) .

APPENDIX A

HISTORICAL FOUNDATIONS

- Psychoanalytical Model
- Phenomenological Model
- Behavioral Model
- Existential Model
- Eclectic Model
- Outline
- Bibliography

APPENDIX A

HISTORICAL FOUNDATIONS

The cognitive gestalt by which the group leader guides his behavior throughout the group process may not always be in his awareness. He may not be able to explicate a theoretical model of either group process or of man's personality, but he is making decisions continuously based on at least some implicit assumptions concerning both the process and the nature of man. Professional pride as well as professional competency would suggest that an understanding of the implications of various models is the basis from which the group leader should work out his own theoretical foundation.

The following comments identify four common models, define the cognitive map of man underlying each model, suggest the parameters of the leader's role, and specify resultant techniques. The functions of group members are identified, followed by goals which are derived from the basic model. A final comment is made concerning various extensions of the model as practiced currently. An outline is provided at the end of the appendix for the reader's convenience.

PSYCHOANALYTICAL MODEL

Cognitive Map of Man

The cognitive map whereby a group leader working from a psychoanalytical frame of reference governs his behavior is, of course, Freud's id-ego-superego. It would be beyond the scope of this chapter to elaborate on this well-known construct. Attention will be given to its applications to the group process.

Group Model

In the psychoanalytical model the group represents the early

217

family constellation. Thus, significant experiences which occurred in each group member's own family, including early childhood events, will be "worked through," and it is hoped that as a result, insight will occur. The assumption is made that if the dynamics of unresolved conflicts are understood, negative effect of the conflict will be removed. It is expected that during group interaction each member will project onto other members his own needs, perceptions, distortions, defenses, etc., which arise from past and present interactions with significant others outside the group. The material produced concerning these conflicts, interactions, and perceptions will be analyzed by the group. It is expected that the group members will learn more ego-controlled behaviors and be less governed by id-controlled behavior. Learning is assumed to be toward the rational and away from the irrational.

Leader's Role

In the psychoanalytical model the leader serves as a symbolic authority figure. He may at times represent father, mother, teacher, or all three simultaneously. He also serves as a symbolic superego against which group members test their own superego precepts. The leader who works within the psychoanalytical framework will help members recall "forgotten" childhood memories, attempt to aid members to reality-test, and to understand dynamics of their own and others' behaviors, eventually verbalizing insights.

Techniques

Techniques derived from the psychoanalytical model include procedures appropriate in individual therapy, such as dream analysis, free association, and recall of early childhood memories. The leader encourages transference, while being alert to counter-transference. He and group members analyze and interpret projective behaviors and defense mechanisms. Verbal behavior of the leader and members includes probing, analyzing, questioning, interpreting and supporting.

Functions of Group Members

In the psychoanalytical model it is the expectation of the group leader that members will function as assistant therapists. Members also function in the roles of each member's early family constellation—siblings, parents, etc. Therefore, the content of the group will often include quarrels, hostilities, and regressive behavior as the members "act out" earlier conflicts.

Group Members' Goals

Members' goals in the psychoanalytical model of the group process are individualized by the therapist according to the needs of each member, but may include desensitization of painful and traumatic past experiences, may clarify for members their "authority" problems, may lessen a member's need to protect his id impulses through use of excessive ego defense mechanisms, may free spontaneity, especially in the area of sexual expression, and may help group members handle identity crises.

Extensions of the Model

One extension of the psychoanalytical model is represented by the marathon format which makes the assumption that under the pressure of continuous group interaction, aided by loss of sleep, the ego defenses of group members are lowered and the core of personality is more available for analysis and insight.

Berne's *Transactional Analysis* (1961) extends the ego of the Freudian construct into three ego states: parent, child, and adult. The transactions which are conducted from each of these three ego states are analyzed in the group process. Various "games" which people "play" in their interactions with each other are identified; this represents much of the content of group work. The life script of each member is clarified, so that behavior can be controlled increasingly by the adult ego state.

PHENOMENOLOGICAL MODEL

Cognitive Map of Man

In the phenomenological model the cognitive map which the group leader uses describes man as a seeking, striving organism with an innate drive toward psychological health. Each group member contains his own "truth" as it is perceived in his idiosyncratic world. The group leader attempts to understand and to enter the phenomenological world of each member and tries to be alert to discrepancies between a member's internalized ideal self and his perceived real self, for this discrepancy is seen as the cause of maladjustment. Psychological health requires harmony between the real and the ideal self.

Group Model

The group environment is designed to create a threat-free oasis where members can examine their self-concepts. The focus of group content is on each individual's perceptions of his world rather than on the relationships between members, per se. Since self-concepts are seen as based primarily in the affective domain, the emphasis of the interaction is on *feelings* rather than on ideas.

Leader's Role

The leader in the phenomenological group attempts to create and maintain a threat-free, permissive atmosphere through his own expressions of acceptance, unconditional regard, and respect. He helps members enter each other's phenomenological world and he attempts to make members aware of their self-concepts by responding to *feelings,* both overt and covert, and by encouraging congruency between feelings and behavior. The leader provides a model of congruency.

Techniques

To label behaviors which follow from the phenomenological model "techniques" is a misnomer, for the group leader mainly exhibits an *attitude* of caring, accepting, and understanding. He understands the idiosyncratic worlds of members. He gains this understanding through intensive, skilled listening, and his chief speech patterns are reflections of feelings, clarification of feelings and ideas, acceptance statements, and unstructured general leads. He performs a linking function as he attempts to help members perceive contradictions between their ideal and their real selves. He consistently responds to conative (affective) content rather than to cognitive content. The group situation is left unstructured deliberately so as to create an ambiguous situation in which group members can explore their own phenomenological fields. The leader may use techniques of immediate feedback via videotape so as to help members meet their "real" selves. He also may use sensory experiences to increase members' awareness of ongoing visceral processes and emotional reactions.

Functions of Group Members

The members of the phenomenological group serve as mirrors in which group participants can check perceptions, distortions, values, etc. Members are encouraged to "care" for other members so that the natural growth forces toward goodness can be released; members provide "human nourishment" for one another.

Group Members' Goals

The goals of the nondirective phenomenological group is the maximum self-actualization of each member. This is achieved by bringing conative processes into awareness so that each member is able to experience another dimension of his living. The innate drive toward the good is released in each member.

Extensions of the Model

Early basic encounter groups were based on the phenomenological model, and current "sensitivity" groups seem based on similar assumptions concerning the nature of man. The Western Behavioral Science Institute's Encountertapes (Tape-recorder-led groups) published by Bell and Howell assume that leaderless groups are satisfactory, and thus must make the assumption of the phenomenologists that man is by nature "good."

BEHAVIORAL MODEL

Cognitive Map of Man

The behavioral model conceptualizes man as a reactive organism: Stimulus, bond, Response. The emphasis is on the "S" and the "R" and these are observable. Man can be shaped to conform to desired behavior through reinforcement techniques.

Group Model

The group process can be used to reinforce desired behaviors under the group leader's direction. The group is the social microcosm which represents the societal macrocosm, and the assumption is made that learning appropriate behavior in the former will generalize to the latter. Roles must be learned, and the group is seen as providing a learning situation where new ways of behaving can be experienced.

Leader's Role

The role of the leader in the behavioral model is to shape members' behaviors.

Techniques

The use of reinforcement by the group leader is consistent in the behavioral model. He will attend selectively—using both verbal and nonverbal feedback to respond to those behaviors he perceives as desirable. "Role modeling" through audio tape is used to provide an example of appropriate behavior. The verbalization of the leader will include approval, disapproval, and leading questions; it will stress operational specificity and cognitive content. The group leader will use his own behavior as a reinforcement model. He also will serve as a source of factual information and a source of value judgments.

Functions of Group Members

Group members reinforce desired behavior in others under the guidance of the group leader.

Group Members' Goals

In the behavioral model group goals are in terms of enculturation rather than individuation, i.e., adjustment to the school setting, increased vocational exploration, educational adjustment, etc. Objectives, however, would be very specific for each member and would be couched in operational terms. The emphasis would be on observable behavior both in and out of the group.

Extensions of the Model

John Krumboltz's "Behavioral Counseling Groups" (1964) are based on a behavioral model of man. Leaders and members together specify desired behaviors; the leader reinforces these behaviors, and primarily attempts to enculturate.

EXISTENTIAL MODEL

Cognitive Map of Man

The Existential model is based on a philosophical rather than a psychological view of Man. Man is seen as existing with no "givens," and his task in life is to define himself through his creations (actions). As he experiences Existential Moments he becomes more and more aware of himself as a person. These events, Existential Moments, begin to occur in early adolescence, and from this time on each man is responsible totally for all his actions. Henceforth, he is condemned to freedom to choose both for himself and all Man. Because of this profound freedom, each of us suffers a human loneliness and anguish. We can assuage our loneliness through the encounter as we relate to one another I-to-Thou.

Group Model

The group exists in the only relevance—the here and the now—and exists for the only relevancy—the I-Thou relationship. Each group member makes his statement about himself through interfacing with others as authentically as possible. The uniqueness of the group process lies in the opportunity it provides for multiple

223

feedback and for multiple encounters. Confrontation is seen as the most productive level of interaction.

Leader's Role

The role of the leader in the Existential model is I-to-Thou in interaction. He risks himself through his authentic relating to group members. He attempts to focus content on the "here and now" rather than on the "there and then." He interacts on a personal level, is open and known, rather than anonymous and knowing. In his verbal behavior he will return consistently to the existent moment, will reflect both feelings and ideas, will link, clarify, make risk-taking statements which center risk in himself, and constantly share himself with group members.

Techniques

The Existentialist group leader will make frequent use of confrontation, but will not attack. He attempts to help members clarify alternatives which pave the way for action choices outside the group. These action possibilities will be specific. He uses interaction techniques to generate immediate productive experiences for group members. The leader's self is the main technique which is ethically available to the counselor. His risk-taking centers on self.

Group Members' Goals

The group members' goals of the Existential model are to clarify self-definitions, to extend potentials, and to extend abilities to sustain intimacy, i.e., encounters. The group functions to alleviate man's essential loneliness through emphatic feedback. The group helps members to attain authenticity more consistently, and each member strives toward self-actualization. Members experience increased awareness of their essential state of freedom and become more and more aware of the attendant responsibility. The group attempts to help each member increase the choices he makes in awareness.

224

Extensions of the Model

Carl Rogers' current Basic Encounter Groups (Hart and Tomlinson, 1970) seem derived from an Existential frame of reference. Glasser (1966) emphasizes the concepts of responsibility and reality-testing which are consonant with Existentialist philosophy. Gestalt (Fagan and Shepherd, 1970; Perls, 1970) approaches, which focus on the here and now, are consistent with the Existentialist approach to group processes.

ECLECTIC MODEL

In the final analysis each group leader must formulate his own model which will be unique to him. Thus, in a sense, each leader is eclectic. The eclecticism, however, must stem from a thorough grounding in theoretical formulation, not from inadequate intellectual preparation. The effective leader will develop his own leadership style—the one most consonant with his strengths and limitations. It is hoped that this volume will facilitate the process.

OUTLINE

PSYCHOANALYTICAL MODEL

Cognitive Map of Man: Id, ego, superego.

Group Model:

1. Group represents family.
2. Significant experiences worked through.
3. Basic assumption: if dynamics of unresolved conflicts are understood, then negative cathexis of conflict is removed.
4. Members project onto other members interactions with significant others outside the group.
5. Materials from projections are analyzed; behavior becomes more ego-controlled than id-controlled, or rational rather than irrational.

Leader's Role:

1. To serve as symbolic authority figure.
2. To serve as symbolic superego.
3. To help members recall "forgotten" childhood memories.
4. To aid insight through verbalization.

Group Leadership

Techniques:
1. Dream Analysis.
2. Encourage transference, be alert to counter-transference.
3. Free association.
4. Analyze and interpret projective behavior.
5. Analyze and interpret defense mechanisms.
6. Verbal behavior: Probing, analyzing, questioning, inter-preting, supporting.

Functions of Group Members:
1. Serve as assistant therapists.
2. Serve in roles of each member's early family constellation—siblings, parents, etc.

Group Members' Goals:
1. To desensitize painful/traumatic past experiences.
2. To clarify "authority" hangups.
3. To lessen members' needs to protect id through ego defense mechanisms.
4. To free spontaneity, especially in area of sexual expression.
5. To help group members handle identity crises.

Extensions of Model:
1. Bach (1967) : Marathon format.
2. Berne (1966) : Transactional Analysis.
3. Moreno (1945) : Psychodrama, Sociodrama (Spectator theory) .

PHENOMENOLOGICAL MODEL

Cognitive Map of Man:
1. Seeking, striving organism with innate drive toward mental health.
2. Imbalance because of discrepancy between ideal and real selves.
3. Truth is perceived idiosyncratically.

Group Model:
1. Threat-free environment where members examine self-concepts.
2. Focus on individual's perception of world.
3. Emphasis on affect rather than cognition.

Leader's Role:
1. Create and maintain a threat-free, permissive atmosphere through own behavior.
2. Help members enter each other's phenomenological world.
3. Make members aware of their self-concepts by responding to *feelings* (overt and covert) and encouraging congruency between feelings and behavior

Techniques:
1. Verbalize feelings, responding to conative content.
2. Transmit caring through verbalizing understanding which is gained through intensive, skilled listening.
3. Verbal behavior: Reflection, clarification, linking, acceptance statements, general leads. Avoid structuring comments.
4. Deliberately create ambiguous, unstructured group environment so group members can create own phenomenological fields.
5. Use of "focused feedback" through videotape to help members meet selves.
6. Use of sensory experience to increase awareness of visceral processes.

Functions of Group Members:
1. Serve as mirrors in which group members can check their perceptions, distortions, values, etc.
2. Transmit "caring" of other members so that natural growth forces toward "goodness" can be released. Members provide "human nourishment" to each other.

Group Members' Goals:
1. Maximum self-actualization of each member.
2. Bring conative processes into awareness.

BEHAVIORAL MODEL

Cognitive Map of Man:
S-R with emphasis on "S" and "R."

Group Model:
1. Laboratory setting used to reinforce desired behaviors under leader's direction.
2. Social microcosm representing societal macrocosm.

227

Group Leadership

Leader's Role:

1. Shape members' behaviors.

Techniques:

1. Reinforce desired behavior through "attending" selectively— use verbal and nonverbal feedback as reinforcers.
2. "Role modeling" through audiotape. (Krumboltz and Thoresen, 1964).
3. Verbal behavior: Approval, disapproval, leading questions, emphasizing cognitive content, emphasizing operational specificity.
4. Use systems analysis approach to problem-solve.
5. Use own behavior as reinforcement model.
6. Provide information.

Functions of Group Members:

To reinforce other members' behaviors under guidance of group leader.

Group Members' Goals

1. Very specific for each member.
2. Specified in operational terms by group leader before group begins.
3. Emphasis on *observable* behavior in and out of group.

Extension of Model:

Krumboltz's "Vocational Guidance Groups," 1964.

EXISTENTIAL MODEL

Cognitive Map of Man:

1. Man exists with no "givens"; must define self.
2. Man condemned to freedom to choose for himself and all Man.

Group Model:

1. Group exists in the "here and now."
2. Group exists for I-Thou relationship.
3. Members make statements about selves through interfacing as authentically as possible.
4. Uniqueness of group in feedback and encounter.

Leader's Role:

1. Opens self I-to-Thou as model.

2. Risks self through sharing self in creating encounters.
3. Through verbalizations keeps focus on here and now rather than on there and then.
4. Through verbalization keeps focus on I-to-Thou rather than he and it.
5. Verbal behavior: Returns constantly to existing moment, reflects feelings and ideas, links, clarifies, makes risk-taking statements, centers risk on self.

Techniques:
1. Frequent use of confrontation, avoids attack.
2. Clarification of alternatives to pave way for action choices.
3. Action possibilities specified.
4. Self is main instrument ethically available to counselor.

Functions of Group Members:
1. To relate to each other on I-to-Thou basis
2. To extend life spaces of members.
3. To provide human nourishment.

Group Goals:
1. To clarify self-definitions of members.
2. To extend abilities of members to sustain intimacy (encounters).
3. To alleviate members' essential loneliness through empathic feedback.
4. To assist members in reaching authentic behavior more frequently.
5. Self-actualization of each member.
6. To make each member more aware of his essential state of freedom with its attendant responsibility.
7. To help members increase numbers of choices they make in awareness.

Extensions of Model:
1. Rogers' current Basic Encounter Groups, 1970.
2. Gestalt, 1970.
3. Extensional model (Bates & Johnson, 1970).

ECLECTIC MODEL
Cognitive Map of Man: ?

Group Leadership

Group Model: ?
Leader's Role: ?
Techniques: Any and all of above.
Functions of Members: ?
Group Members' Goals: ?
Extensions of Model: Almost any group?

BIBLIOGRAPHY

Bach, George R. "Marathon Group Dynamics: I. Some Functions of the Professional Group Facilitator." *Psychological Reports.* 1967, 20, 995-999.

Berne, Eric. *Principles of Group Treatment.* New York: Oxford University Press, 1966.

Bradford, Leland; Gibb, Jack; and Benne, Kenneth. *T-Group Theory and Laboratory Method: Innovation in Re-education.* New York: Wiley and Sons, 1964.

Encounter Tapes, Leader-less Group Tapes, Western Behavioral Science Institute, La Jolla, Ca.

Fagan, Joen, and Shepherd, Irma Lee. *Gestalt Therapy Now.* Palo Alto: Science and Behavior Books, 1970.

Glasser, William, and Iverson, Norman. *Large Group Counseling.* Los Angeles: The Reality Press, 1966.

Hart, J.T., and Tomlinson, T.M. *New Directions in Client-Centered Therapy.* Boston: Houghton Mifflin, 1970.

Krumboltz, John, and Thoresen, Carl. "The Effect of Behavioral Counseling in Group and Individual Settings on Information-Seeking Behavior." *Journal of Counseling Psychology,* 1964, 11, 324-335.

Moreno, J.L., ed. *Group Psychotherapy.* Beacon, N.Y.: Beacon Press, 1945.

Otto, Herbert, ed. *Explorations in Human Potentialities.* Springfield, Ill.: Thomas, 1966.

Perls, Frederick S. *Gestalt Therapy Verbatim.* Palo Alto, Ca.: Science and Behavior Books, 1970.

Rogers, Carl R. "The Process of the Basic Encounter Group," in *New Directions in Client-Centered Therapy.* Hart and Tomlinson. Boston: Houghton Mifflin Co., 1970.

APPENDIX B

DEFINITIONS OF GROUP PROCESSES

I. INSIDE PUBLIC INSTITUTIONS
- Small Group Instruction
  Definition and Goals · Dynamics · Training
  Requirements · Specialized Materials
- Small Group Activity (Task Groups)
  Definition and Goals · Dynamics · Training
  Requirements · Specialized Materials
- Group Guidance
  Definition and Goals · Dynamics · Training
  Requirements · Specialized Materials
- Group Counseling
  Definition and Goals · Dynamics · Training
  Requirements · Specialized Materials

II. OUTSIDE PUBLIC INSTITUTIONS:
- T-Groups
  Definition and Goals · Dynamics · Training
  Requirements · Specialized Materials
- Sensitivity Training Groups (Encounter Groups)
  Definition and Goals · Dynamics · Training
  Requirements · Specialized Materials
- Therapy Groups and Marathons
  Definition and Goals · Dynamics · Training
  Requirements · Specialized Materials

APPENDIX B

DEFINITIONS OF GROUP PROCESSES

I. INSIDE PUBLIC INSTITUTIONS—DIRECTED TOWARD STUDENTS

SMALL GROUP INSTRUCTION:

Definition and Goals: Small group instruction is appropriate to transmit content materials which are commonly found in a school's curriculum. The setting ordinarily is the classroom and the group is the usual class. The leader has in mind a body of cognitive material he wishes to be learned; also, he has objectives concerning attitudes toward the material.

Dynamics: The dynamics which are activated are subgrouping of the larger class, face-to-face discussion within the small sub-groups, feedback to the class group through subgroup reporters, and maximum participation of each class member. The assumption is that the dynamics of verbalized interaction by members enhance learning. The opportunity for members to be active, rather than passive, participants is part of small group instruction.

Training Requirements: The teacher can successfully lead small instructional groups using skills inherent in teaching. He should draw on his training of organizing, planning ahead, and presenting instructions so that the small groups have clearly-defined goals and understand clearly-defined objectives and procedures. Such skills should be developed as a result of the teacher's professional education, which ought to have included work in classroom group dynamics.

Specialized Materials: Small group instructional procedures are presented in Hill's *Learning Thru Discussion* (1969) and by Randolph's *Self-Enhancing Education* (1968). Ways of organizing groups into subgroups using an adaptation by Gibb (1951) of "Phillip's 66' method are summarized along with Hill's and Randolph's materials in Appendix D.

232

SMALL GROUP ACTIVITY (TASK GROUPS) :

Definition and Goals: Small group activity groups are task-oriented groups with a group goal which consists of creating a product or completing a project. This might involve planning a school dance, managing student government, preparing a committee report, or making campaign posters for a class election. The end product is viewed as valuable, but the process is of equal worth.

Dynamics: The dynamics of problem-solving, trial-and-error experiences, and skills of committee work, such as reaching a concensus through discussion, are involved. The process of decision-making and awareness of the responsibility for the decisions are experienced. Face-to-face discussion with airing of opposing views and opinions is encouraged. Sufficient time for all members to participate is essential. The dynamics of brainstorming may be used to release creative forces in members (See Appendix D). Members may learn group skills such as gatekeeping, harmonizing, initiating, clarifying, informing, summarizing, reality-testing, compromising, and consensus-testing and may learn to deal with such blocking group roles as aggressor, dominator, avoidance behaviors, and hidden agendas (Benne and Sheats, 1948) (See Appendix D). The dynamics of the various phases of the group process characteristic of task-oriented groups should be understood by the group leader. An awareness of the probable stages through which a group will move enables a group leader to comprehend the significance of events as they occur in sequential steps.

Training Requirements: The type of training given to the teacher in his professional education should be supplemented by some specialized knowledge of the dynamics of task group processes. Personality characteristics, such as ability to tolerate some confusion, patience with the democratic process, and a background in interaction analysis (Amidon and Hough, 1967), should enable the leader to function adequately in the small activity group.

Specialized Materials: Bales (1950) provides an analysis of group interaction patterns which should be mastered by the classroom teacher. Bales and Strodtbeck (1967) present a helpful analysis of the phases of group interaction. Another conceptual model for stages

233

of the group process is presented by Schutz (1958). Benne and Sheats's (1948) early work provides a useful paradigm for understanding dynamics of problem-solving groups in relation to the roles of group members. The process of brainstorming is an excellent group technique which stimulates creative thinking (Osborn, 1957). These specialized materials which the group leader of task-oriented groups might find useful are presented in Appendix D.

GROUP GUIDANCE:

Definition and Goals: Group guidance is a method of presenting selected educational/vocational/attitudinal materials to a group usually numbering from 10 to 100. The goal is to impart a specific body of knowledge drawn from the area of pupil personnel services. Ideas and concepts are explored, but attitudes concerning the materials are of equal importance.

The material presented in group guidance usually requires technical knowledge on the part of the leader: for example, vocational information, educational requirements, test interpretation data, study skills knowledge, and graduation requirements.

Dynamics: In part a didactic approach may be used in group guidance, although probably multi-media presentations should be employed to clarify technical aspects of the material being presented: for example, a stanine chart might be used in test interpretation. Frequently a paper and pencil instrument which might include an interest inventory or a diagnostic instrument of study skills is used to provide background for discussion. Small group discussion dynamics should be activated, such as student face-to-face discussions, verbalizations of attitudes and values surrounding the content materials, questions and answers, role-playing, panel discussions, and sociodrama.

Training Requirements: Teaching skills are basic, but the leader of a guidance group also needs to possess a body of specialized technical knowledge concerning educational and vocational areas. This training usually is obtained through the course work required for a credential to perform pupil personnel work. The course work should include group dynamics.

Specialized Materials: A group guidance technique designed to explore the world of work has been created by Robert Hoppock (1968) who works with groups of high school students as they interview employed alumni. Hoppock has a structured procedure around which he builds the group conference (See Appendix D).

Ostrom's *Self Appraisal and Assessment Structure* (1969) is one approach to group guidance which can be applied to various age levels (See Appendix D).

Varenhorst's *Life Career Games* (no date) approach to vocational exploration uses a simulation approach which can be adapted to a variety of settings and a variety of age levels (See Appendix D).

Williams' *Choice or Chance* (1969) is another group guidance procedure; it is directed at vocational exploration with seventh, eighth, and ninth grade students. The materials can be used in a classroom by a teacher-guidance worker team and focus on the decision-making process (See Appendix D).

A group guidance approach to vocational and educational orientation has been formulated by Grossmont District in San Diego County and consists of four interest units: "My High School," "World of Work," "Our Changing World," and "Self Appraisal" (See Appendix D).

GROUP COUNSELING:

Definition and Goals: Group counseling in the public school or institutional setting is a process where a small group of six to twelve students engage in a meaningful multilogue concerning educational, vocational, social, and personal values under the leadership of a competent professional trained in group leadership as defined in this manual. The purpose of the group is to enable students to become more available to the learning process as presented in the setting. The emphasis is on the *individuation* of the member rather than on his *enculturation*. There are no group goals as in group guidance; rather, there are individual objectives for each member of the group which are set by the member in conjunction with the leader at the time of the pre-group interview. A post-group interview is held with each member at the conclusion of the group meetings, and at this time evaluation of progress toward the specified objectives is made.

235

Group Leadership

Dynamics: The group counselor deliberately establishes an unstructured field so as to use tensions which arise from ambiguity; thus, members bring to the group concerns which have root in the affective domain. The group leader uses techniques of reflection of both ideas and feelings, clarifies distortions and contradictions, may or may not summarize, links ideas and feelings, listens intensely for surface and subsurface meanings, may encourage confrontation, and generally focuses on the value systems of participants as they are reflected in life choices. The leader provides an experience where members can test limits through specifying a limited number of sessions—from six to eight—which begin and end on time.

Training Requirements: The leader should have specialized training in leading counseling groups, which includes supervised group leadership. A certification of competency in group counseling leadership should be obtained from an institution of higher learning offering an approved program of counselor education.

Specialized Materials: *It All Has To Do With Identity* by Terry McCarty (1969) is a programmed text designed to help elementary and secondary school children learn to use a counseling group (See Appendix D). It is based on the *Hill Interaction Matrix* (1965).

II. OUTSIDE PUBLIC INSTITUTIONS—DIRECTED TOWARD NON-STUDENTS

T-GROUPS:

Definition and Goals: T-groups or Training Groups are groups conducted by the National Training Laboratories for the express purpose of increasing the effectiveness of institutional and industrial employees through their becoming more sensitive to staff relationships and more sensitive to themselves as interacting beings. The purpose of the group, therefore, is to enable each employee to become a more productive member of the employing institution—usually a business or industry. Enculturation as it involves more efficient employee functioning is the goal, rather than individual personal growth.

Dynamics: T-groups use the "ocean voyage" dynamic of holding groups in a setting removed from the usual environment. Preferred is a comfortable atmosphere which enhances the "shipboard" aura.

Members are cast together for an intense journey of self-exploration. An ambiguous, unstructured field is created so that members can explore how they apply structure to situations and how they approach problems. The group process is examined so that members can become aware of how they interact with others. It is expected that this knowledge will generalize to the work setting. Face-to-face confrontations may occur as the group experiences prolonged stress created by the absence of clear-cut goals and the refusal of the "trainer" to provide structure. Members are expected to express with complete honesty their reactions to and feelings about others in the group. Negative responses will probably precede positive responses.

Training Requirements: The leader should be trained and approved by the National Training Laboratories (NTL) at Bethel, Maine. NTL offers training programs throughout the United States.

Specialized Materials: Dealing with specific procedures of T-groups is beyond the scope of this manual and the reader is referred to Bradford, et al., *T-Group Theory and Laboratory Method: Innovation in Re-Education* (1964).

SENSITIVITY TRAINING GROUPS (ENCOUNTER GROUPS):

Definition and Goals: Sensitivity groups, encounter groups, "feedback" groups, self-actualizing groups, etc., are terms commonly used to describe a type of group which has as its purpose the goal of assisting members to live a richer, more fulfilling life. Such groups are developmental rather than remedial, and members are expected to become more self-actualized as a result of participation in such a group. Usually, no specific model of the self-actualizing person is prescribed, athough Maslow's (1968) paradigm probably would be accepted by most participants.

Dynamics: The facilitator of a sensitivity group attempts to create a feeling of love and acceptance in the group through presenting in himself such a model. A variety of verbal and nonverbal exercises may be used to help members become more aware of their feelings, their bodies, and of each other. Emphasis is on honest and open communication; this is encouraged through the example of the leader

237

and through various exercises.

In the T-group the process itself is examined for understanding of the dynamics involved. In sensitivity groups the relationships among the members and the personal awarenesss of each person toward himself and toward others are emphasized.

The leader reflects feelings, transmits acceptance and unconditional positive regard, and emphasizes empathy among group members. Confrontation may be involved.

Training Requirements: In California a "Marriage and Family Counseling License" with special training in group leadership should be supplemented by experience as a group member. In other states the standards of the state psychological association should provide a basic minimal standard. Professional controls need to be created so that prospective members can obtain information concerning the qualifications of group leaders.

Specialized Materials: There are a variety of types of sensitivity groups, and each uses differing approaches. Esalen, Kairos, and Topanga Canyon are California centers which provide group membership experiences presented from many different points of view. The addresses of these centers are listed at the end of this chapter. *Please Touch* (Howard, 1970) provides a reference of "Growth Centers and Kindred Establishments" throughout the United States. The reader is referred also to the chapter in this manual entitled "The Misuse of Groups."

THERAPY GROUPS AND MARATHONS:

Definition and Goals: Therapy groups are organized for the purpose of correcting neurotic or psychotic behaviors which impede an individual's functioning The purpose may be a minor or a major restructuring of personality, and approaches vary depending on the theoretical orientation of the leader. A marathon is an intensive group experience with the group interacting without interruption over an extended period of time.

Dynamics: The dynamics utilized in therapy groups also vary according to the theoretical orientation of the leader. The reader is referred to the chapter in this manual on theoretical frameworks of groups.

Training Requirements: Training for leading therapy groups is highly specialized and usually long-term; also, training requires an advanced degree. Personal therapy on the part of the leader, both individual and group, is a basic prerequisite to entering training as a group therapy leader.

Specialized Materials: The magnitude of the materials available and the extent of the variety of approaches to group therapy make a discussion of possible specialized materials beyond the scope of this manual. For this reason no attempt has been made to provide a bibliography.

APPENDIX C

RESOURCE LITERATURE FOR DIFFERENT TYPES OF GROUPS

I. INSIDE PUBLIC INSTITUTIONS—Directed Toward Students

Small Group Instruction

Gibb, Jack R.; Platts, Grace N.; and Miller, Lorraine F., *Dynamics of Participative Groups.* St. Louis, Mo.: Swift, 1951.

Hill, Wm. Fawcett. *Learning Thru Discussion (LTD).* Beverly Hills: Sage Publications, 1962.

Randolph, Norma; Howe, William; Achterman, Elizabeth. *Self-Enhancing Education.* Palo Alto, Ca.: Stanford Press, 1966.

Small Group Activity (Task Groups)

Amidon, Edmund J., and Hough, John B. *Interaction Analysis: Theory, Research and Application.* Reading, Mass.: Addison Wesley, 1967.

Bales, Robert F. *Interaction Process Analysis.* Cambridge, Mass.: Addison Wesley, 1950.

Bales, Robert F., and Strodtbeck, Fred L. "Phases in Group Problem Solving," in *Interaction Analysis: Theory, Research and Application.* Reading, Mass.: Addison Wesley, 1967, pp. 89-102.

Benne, Kenneth D., and Sheats, Paul. "Functional Roles of Group Members." *Journal of Social Issues,* Vol. 4, No. 2, 1948, pp. 41-49.

Osborn, Alex F. *Applied Imagination: Principles and Procedures of Creative Thinking.* New York: Charles Scribner's Sons, 1957, p. 84.

Phillips, Gerald M. *Communication and the Small Group.* New York: Bobbs-Merrill, 1966.

Schutz, William C. *FIRO: A Three-Dimensional Theory of Interpersonal Behavior.* New York: Rinehart & Co., 1958.

Group Leadership

Group Guidance

Hoppock, Robert. *Questions for Group Conferences with Employed Alumni*. New York: New York Univ. School of Education, 1968.

Ostrom, Stanley R. *Self Appraisal and Assessment Structure*. 1953 Colleen Drive, Los Altos, Calif. 94222, 1969.

San Diego County Department of Education. *Planning Your Future*. Superintendent of Schools, San Diego County, 6401 Linda Vista Road, San Diego, Ca. Sept. 1965.

Varenhorst, Barbara. *Life Career Games*. Palo Alto: Guidance Department, Palo Alto Unified School District, 25 Churchill Ave., Palo Alto, Ca., n.d.

Williams, Robert. *Choice or Chance: Career Planning and Development Emphasizing The Decision-Making Process*. Oakland Unified School District, Oakland, Ca., 1969.

Group Counseling

McCarty, Terry. *It All Has To Do With Identity*. Beverly Hills: Sage Publications, 1969.

II. OUTSIDE PUBLIC INSTITUTIONS—Directed Toward Non-Students

T-Groups

Bradford, Leland, et al. *T-Group Theory and Laboratory Method: Innovation in Re-Education*. New York: John Wiley & Sons, 1964.

Gottschalk, Louis A., and Pattison, E. Mansell. "Psychiatric Perspectives on T-Groups and the Laboratory Movement: An Overview." *American Journal of Psychiatry*, Dec. 1969.

Maslow, Abraham H. *Toward A Psychology of Being*. New York: Van Nostrand Reinhold, 1968.

Sensitivity Training Groups (Encounter Groups)

Esalen Institute, Big Sur, Ca. 93920. Also: 776 Union St., San Francisco, Ca. 94123.

Howard, Jane. *Please Touch*. New York: McGraw-Hill, 1970.

Kairos, P.O. Box 350 Rancho Santa Fe, Ca. 92067.

Topanga Canyon Center for Human Development, 11489 Chandler Blvd., North Hollywood, Ca. 91601.

APPENDIX D

SPECIALIZED MATERIALS FOR VARIOUS GROUPS

I. INSIDE PUBLIC SCHOOLS—Directed Toward Students

Small Group Instruction

Gibb, Jack R., Platts, Grace N.; and Miller, Lorraine F. *Dynamics of Participative Groups.* Using Phillips 66 Method to Organize for Group Discussion:

J. D. Phillips, Director of Continuing Education, Michigan State, originally designed his *PHILLIPS 66 METHOD* as a means of gaining maximum participation from members of a large group. The technique is appropriate for the group leader who has a minimum of group leadership skills, and can be used successfully with groups varying from classroom to auditorium sizes. Members are subgrouped so that each has a chance to become involved in contributing to the larger group. Each member has an opportunity to verbalize his opinions, knowledges, and decisions. The method moves an audience very quickly from passive participants to active, involved contributors, yet no one is "put on the spot."

The group dynamics of arranging for face-to-face interaction are utilized. The area on the *Hill Interaction Matrix* (Hill, 1965) will primarily be the Conventional Cells and may range from Topic to Group, to Personal, and perhaps to Relationship.

The group leader begins the interaction by making a clear statement of the task, which might be a decision to reach, a problem to discuss, or plans to formulate for a variety of circumstances. Time should be spent on making the task clear to the members of the audience so that each understands the objective of the small group interaction. It also must be very clear that each group is expected to present a report to the larger group at the end of the small group discussions. The leader then divides the large group into subgroups of six each, by numbering off one through six, and then grouping each set together. The leader suggests that first names be used so that an informal atmosphere is created, rather than a "Town Meeting" parliamentary procedure atmosphere which might inhibit free, creative discussion. Members should have some commitment to the problem and the leader should use his introductory remarks to elicit this commitment. Members are seated as comfortably as possible, preferably in a circle.

Subgroups are instructed to select a leader who will be time keeper and who will be responsible for seeing that each member has a chance to contribute. The original format calls for a time allotment of six minutes with six members, but of course the time and size of subgrouping should be adjusted to the needs of the situation. The group is also instructed to choose a recorder/spokesman who will make note of the group's ideas and will report back to the larger group. Each group is asked to follow these specific directions:

1. As soon as the subgroups are formed, each member spends one minute thinking of his best ideas concerning the task at hand before the discussion begins.

2. After the silent "brainstorming," each member spends one minute presenting his ideas to the subgroup in a "go around."

3. A free discussion of the ideas follows in the subgroup.

4. A summary is made by the recorder/spokesman and read to the subgroup to see that he has recorded the best thinking of the group.

One minute before the time limit previously set by the large group leader, he warns the subgroups that there are only sixty seconds left for discussion. He then closes the discussion and the large group is reformed. Each reporter/spokesman presents his group's ideas to the large group and the large group leader asks someone to write the ideas on the board as each report is made. It is vital that each recorder/spokesman has an opportunity to be heard, although each is asked to avoid duplication if a previous group has presented the same idea. Also, the ideas should be written for the large group exactly as the subgroup recorder/spokesman presents them, without editing or evaluation. The large group decides which of the ideas they wish to use or pursue. It is the leader's responsibility that none of the contributions is denigrated in any way.

Hill, Wm. Fawcett. *Learning Thru Discussion (LTD)* :

This small paperback is a guide for leaders and members of discussion groups in which the purpose is to transmit a body of knowledge available in written form. Hill's method replaces the traditional lecture method in which the teacher serves as expert with the discussion method whereby the teacher serves as resource consultant. The learner assumes an active, seeking role.

Hill presents nine specific steps which the group leader is to present to the learners who are required to follow these steps in specific order. *Step One* is for the group to define terms and concepts so that there will be a common understanding of meanings. *Step Two* requires that group members state the general meaning of the author's message. (Hill's method presumes that group members prepare for the discussion by reading the assigned materials outside of class.) *Step Three* asks the group to identify the major themes of sub-topics in the assigned materials. Thus, the emphasis is on what the author has to say, rather than on the opinions of the students at this point. *Step Four,* the crucial step in the method, concerns the allocation of time which is to be devoted to discussing each of the identified sub-topics. *Step Five* deals with the actual discussion of the major themes and subtopics with strict adherence to the time allotments agreed upon in Step Four. *Step Six* asks group members to make a conscious effort to relate learnings in the assignment to ideas and concepts acquired in previous meetings or in other learning situations. Thus, it is hoped that knowledges will be integrated and consequently retained. *Step Seven* calls for an application of the material to other areas of the participants' lives—personal as well as intellectual. *Step Eight* concerns an evaluation of the author's presentation and, at this point the personal reactions of the students are programmed into the method. The final step—*Step Nine*—allows for evaluation of the group and individual performance: that is, what went well, what was useful, and where did the group err?

Hill lists criteria for a good group and identifies functional and non-functional roles of group members. The manual is very specific concerning the role of the group leader (teacher) and the role of the group member (student). An outline is presented for student use, and the manual concludes with a post-meeting "Reaction Sheet."

Randolph, Norma. *Self Enhancing Education (SEE)*:

The training manual for SEE is designed to accompany the text, *Self Enhancing Education.* In the training manual are presented ten units which deal with ways teachers interact with children in the classroom. The units present learning opportunities around a statement of the problem; the purpose of the unit; the activity designed around the problem; the thinking processes involved in the activity; the social skill needed and/or developed; and means of evaluation. Each unit presents a number of learning opportunities carefully described. Throughout the units, dynamics of group processes are activated. Although focus is on elementary school children, the procedures could be adapted for any grade level.

Small Group Activity (Task Groups)

Bales, Robert. *Interaction Process Analysis*:

Bales, a pioneer in interaction process analysis, has developed categories into which group acts can be ordered. His suggestions are interesting, but for the group leader of task-oriented groups, only a general indication of Bales' paradigm is necessary. This classification system involves a division of contributions into "task" and "socio-emotional" categories. Task contributions include such areas as "gives suggestion," "gives fact," "asks for fact," "asks for opinion," "asks for suggestion," etc. Socio-emotional contributions cover "shows solidarity," "tension release," "agrees," "disagrees," "tension mounts," "shows aggressions." By classifying each contribution, verbal or nonverbal, under one of these headings and then analyzing the relationship of the total output of each member compared to the pattern for the group, insight may be gained into the climate of the group and the influence of the individual members. The interactionist system of analysis requires trained observers to classify with some degree of consistency.

Bales, Robert, and Strodtbeck, Fred L. *Phases in Group Problem Solving*:

The group leader who is working with task groups may find research findings of Bales and Strodtbeck useful as a general paradigm for predicting *phases* which can be anticipated as a group goes through a problem-solving process. These writers found that the group process tends to move through time from a relative emphasis on (1) *orientation problems* where the facts relevant to the decision to be made are clear. Information is requested; opinions and suggestions are offered as group members attempt to orient themselves to the task. Once orientation problems are cleared away, the group tends to move to (2) *problems of evaluation,* where group members express various values and interests concerning the facts of the situation and express opinions regarding how the proposed course of action is to be judged. From the evaluation phase, the group tends to move to (3) *problems of control,* if there is pressure for a group decision and the expectation of further action. The control phase involves giving suggestions, determining direction, asking for suggestions, and encouraging discussion concerning possible problem-solving behaviors. The control phase involves the group assigning tasks, making decisions, and performing activities.

The group leader may find this paradigm of expected phases in a group problem-solving experience useful when working with this type of group. Awareness that a group will, in all probability, move from *orientation* to *evaluation* to *control* will provide the leader with a general "road map" of the group problem-solving territory.

Benne, Kenneth D., and Sheats, Paul. *Functional Roles of Group Members*:

The functional roles of group members have been identified by Benne and Sheats, and leaders of task groups may find it helpful to recognize which of the member roles are facilitating and which are blocking. It is understood, of course, that group members enact more than one role throughout a session, as does the leader.

Facilitating Roles:

  1. The *initiator-contributor* suggests to the group new ideas re-

garding the group problem or goal. The idea may concern a new goal, or a definition of the problem, or a new procedure, or a new way of organizing for the task.

2. The *information-seeker* asks for clarification of terms and ideas and for more information and facts relevant to the idea being discussed. He should perform this function for clarification within the group rather than for his own ego needs, or his role becomes that of a blocker.

3. The *opinion-seeker* may seek the position of other members concerning values of the group undertaking.

4. The *information-giver* offers facts or generalizations which are needed by the group.

5. The *elaborator* spells out suggestions in terms of examples or develops meanings; offers a rationale for suggestions previously made; and tries to deduce how an idea or suggestion would work out if adopted by the group.

6. The *opinion-giver* states his belief or opinion concerning material brought up in the group.

7. The *dominator* tries to assert authority or superiority in manipulating the group or certain members of the group. This domination may take the form of flattery, or asserting a superior status, giving directions authoritatively, interrupting, etc.

8. The *help-seeker* attempts to call forth sympathy responses from other group members or from the entire group through expressions of personal depreciation, insecurity, or, in general, "kick-me" behaviors.

9. The *special interest-pleader* speaks for the "small businessman," the "grass roots" community, the "special student," etc., usually cloaking his own prejudices or biases in the stereotype which best fits his own needs.

Benne and Sheats also identify group building and maintenance roles which are designed to maintain, regulate, and strengthen the group as a group. The *encourager* who praises, agrees, transmits warmth and solidarity performs this task; as does the *harmonizer,* who pours oil on troubled waters; and the *compromiser,* who admits his errors and offers compromises; or the gate-keeper, who attempts to keep comunication channels open through his regulatory statements. The *standard-setter* also can be helpful as he attempts to express standards for the group. The *group process-observer* who keeps records of various aspects of the group process can be helpful, as is the *follower,* who goes along with the movement of the group, serving as an audience in group discussion and decision.

Osborn, Alex F. *Brainstorming*:

"Brainstorming" is a concept designed to develop new ideas through the creation of an uninhibited atmosphere which engenders spontaneity and teamwork. It was originally developed by Alex Osborn (1957) to counteract negative conference thinking. The technique may be used with small or large groups, but usually a group of twelve members is most functional.

In a brainstorming session the problem must be clearly stated, be brief, specific, and stimulating. The purpose and procedures of brainstorming as a small group method to collect creative ideas should be clear to all group members since even one non-brainstormer can inhibit the process. Each member should understand that the purpose is to stimulate a free flow of ideas from all members without regard to critical threat and without regard to relevance. No contribution is ignored and no flight of fancy is barred. Osborn suggests four basic rules:

1. *Criticism is ruled out.* Adverse judgment of ideas must be withheld until later.

2. *Freewheeling is encouraged.* The wilder the idea, the better; it is easier to tame down than to think up.

3. *Quantity is desired.* The greater the number of ideas, the more the likelihood of winners.

4. *Combination and improvement are sought.* In addition to contributing ideas of their own, participants should suggest how ideas of others can be turned into *better* ideas, or how two or more ideas can be joined into still another idea.

The leader begins the brainstorming session by explaining the ground rules that every idea is acceptable, no matter how absurd or silly it may seem. No evaluation, either verbal or nonverbal, is permitted during the creative brainstorming period. Freewheeling ideas are encouraged—the more and the wilder the better. More coherent ideas normally follow. Free association to other ideas is encouraged. One idea stimulates another and another and another. During the fantasy flight, anything goes. A time limit for this stage of the discussion should be set, however, at the beginning of the meeting, and a three-minute warning should be given by the leader.

The leader, or recorder, lists each idea on a pad as quickly as possible, exactly as given, without editing. A tape recorder is useful as a supplementary record of the brainstorming suggestions.

The session normally begins with an initial spurt of ideas and then slows down. If silence is allowed by the leader, new ideas are usually forthcoming.

Once the brainstorming period is ended, the group can categorize and evaluate the suggestions, or, if it seems advisable, can divide into subgroups to select ten of the most promising suggestions. When the group reforms, it is the leader's task to act as moderator—summarizing, clarifying, and consolidating threads of thought.

Schutz, William C. *FIRO: A Three-Dimensional Theory of Interpersonal Behavior.* Phases of Group Development:

Schutz developed another model of the *phases of group development* somewhat similar to that presented by Bales and Strodbeck (1967). Schutz (1958) believes that every interpersonal relation follows the same course of development and resolution. His *inclusion* phase begins with the formation of the group. This involves being in or out of the group, establishing one's self as a specific individual, and seeing if one is going to receive attention. Anxiety levels may be high at this point and may lead to excessive talking, extreme withdrawal, exhibitionism, and recitation of biographies and other previous experiences. During this phase the problem of commitment to the group is present as each member is going through the process of deciding to what degree he will become a member of the group— how much he will invest. If the leader provides the group with a decision to make at the outset, the inclusion phase may be facilitated. One such decision might be whether or not to take minutes or to have refreshments, etc. As the group discusses these issues, members are able to respond to one another, learn about each other and the leader, and define their roles in the group. These discussions perform an important function, and the skilled leader will make provisions for them early in the group's life.

After the problems of inclusion have been sufficiently resolved, *control problems* arise. The issue of decision-making procedures, which involve sharing responsibility and distributing power, becomes uppermost in the group process. Characteristic behavior at this stage involves a struggle for leadership (i.e., competition), and discussions concerning rules of procedures, methods of decision-making, and structuring tasks. Anxieties at this stage center around having too much or too little responsibility and too much or too little influence.

Once problems of conrol are solved satisfactorily, *problems of affection* become uppermost. Members are now ready to become emotionally integrated. Characteristic behavior at this stage concerns expressions of positive feelings, direct personal hostility, jealousies, pairing behavior, and, in general, heightened emotional feeling between pairs of people. Members may worry whether they are liked, or whether they are too intimate, or not intimate enough. Each member strives to reach his most comfortable level of affection-giving and affection-receiving.

Schutz points out that the three phases are not separate and distinct, but that at any given stage one of the phases will be emphasized. All three problem areas are always present, throughout the life of the group.

Group Guidance

Hoppock, Robert. *Group Guidance Using Employed Alumni:*

Robert Hoppock designed a structured approach to group guidance. He uses employed alumni as a resource to help students explore the world of work. Hoppock suggests that the guidance worker invite an employed alumnus to meet with small groups of students. The function of the group leader is to guide the interaction between the speaker and the students; the leader places the following outline in the hands of the student participants:

Questions for Group Guidance Using Employed Alumni

—What schools did you attend?

—Did you graduate? Drop out? When?

—What was your first job?

> How did you get it?
>
> What three things did you like best about it? Least?
>
> How long were you there?
>
> Why did you leave?

—What was your next job?

> Same question as above.
>
> Repeat for all subsequent jobs.

—Regarding present job, ask also:

> What time did you go to work this morning?
>
> What was the first thing you did?
>
> How long did that take?

—What did you do next?

> Repeat through the entire day.

—Did you do anything yesterday that was different from what you did today?

—How about the day before yesterday? Last week? Last month?

—What else do you do on your job?

—Of all these various duties, which ones take most of your time?

—What three things do you like best about your job? Least?

—What is the usual starting salary in jobs like yours?

—What qualifications do you need to get the job?

> Age? Sex? Height? Weight? Other physical? Marital status? Tools? License? Aptitudes? Unions? Discrimination? Veterans? Capital?

—Preparation? Minimum? Desirable? Time? Cost? Content? Approved schools? Preferred subjects?

—Supply and demand for workers? Outlook for the future? Advancement?

—Hours? Regular? Overtime? Evenings? Sundays? Holidays?

—Steady or seasonal? Hazards? Marriage rate?

—Anything we should have asked?

You ask us? Thanks.

Ostrom, Stanley R. *Self Appraisal and Assessment Structure*:

Self Appraisal and Assessment Structure has been designed as an instrument to help students look at themselves in a number of vocationally- and educationally-oriented areas. The instrument consists of twelve scales divided into two groups: the first group deals with fields of work and the second deals with abilities or traits important for school success. The student is helped to determine systematically his best fields and his level of attainment in those fields.

The major thrust of the instrument is to help the student produce a self-concept which is realistic, but the focus of the procedure is an appraisal by the student of his abilities *as he sees them* at the present time.

Self-Appraisal and Assessment Structure is a group guidance tool designed for classroom use, to be presented by the teacher or the counselor. A *Manual* ($1.50), one classroom set of scales ($.35 each), and a *Student Handbook* ($.25) which is consumable constitute the necessary materials. Thus, the cost is minimal.

The materials can be incorporated at any grade level and should be combined with a testing program. The procedure is flexible as to time, depending on the depths the teacher or guidance worker wishes to explore. At least two weeks of one class period, however, should be allotted to the program. Materials may be obtained by writing Dr. Stanley R. Ostrom, 1953 Colleen Drive, Los Altos, 94022 (Tel. (415) 968-4295).

Varenhorst, Barbara. *Life Career Game*:

The *Life Career Game* kit is published by the Guidance Department of the Palo Alto Unified School District and is designed for use in junior high and high schools to help students explore vocational choices and vocational values with focus on self-concept development. The procedure utilized in the games is a simulation approach which can be used either by the teacher or guidance worker, but training in the technique is necessary. The unit can run from two to six weeks using one class period a day. The price of the kit is $6.00 and the

253

Group Leadership

material may be duplicated locally.

Williams, Robert. *Choice or Chance: Career Planning and Development Emphasizing the Decision-Making Process*:

The "Choice or Chance" approach to group guidance takes junior high school students through a nine-week unit of decision-making concerning career planning and development. The seventh grade unit concerns self-appraisal; the eighth grade unit deals with an in-depth exploration of the world of work; and the ninth grade unit explores vocations. Provision is made at each grade level for students to experience the decision-making process.

The materials may be ordered from the Oakland Public Schools (Ca.), Department of Counseling and Occupational Information, Attention: Dr. Robert C. Williams, Director of Counseling.

San Diego County Department of Education. *Planning Your Future*:

A group guidance procedure for use by either the teacher or guidance worker in orienting junior high school students to their future in senior high school has been formulated by several San Diego County school districts in cooperation with the San Diego Department of Education, and is titled *Planning Your Future*. The materials are grouped into four units: "Self-Appraisal," "Our Changing World," "The World of Work," and "My High School." Each unit can be used separately from the others. Each includes an overview, a listing of objectives and learning experiences to achieve the objectives, descriptions of teacher activities and student activities, and a noting of materials needed.

The materials were developed specifically for the Grossmont Union High School District and the elementary school districts contained therein, but the learning experiences suggested could be adapted to local guidance needs. The material may be ordered through San Diego County Department of Education, San Diego County, 6401 Linda Vista Road, San Diego, Ca. 92111—Pupil Personnel Services.

Group Counseling

McCarty, Terry. *It All Has To Do With Identity*.

It All Has To Do With Identity is a downward extension of the *Hill Interaction Matrix*. It is a programmed manual designed to be used with young people capable of reading and comprehending at a sixth grade level or above and it attempts to teach group members how to use the group process. The manual orients members toward recognizing the forms of interaction most helpful for understanding self. The assumption McCarty makes is that group members can and should be taught to use the group process. His manual can be purchased; the reader is referred to the bibliography presented in Appendix C for publication data.

All of the above-mentioned publications are included in the Appendix C Bibliography.

APPENDIX E

SO YOU ARE GOING TO BE IN GROUP COUNSELING: AN INDUCTION TOOL FOR STUDENTS

Pamphlet for Students

To the Student:

This pamphlet was written to help answer some of your questions about group counseling. You will find included some questions that have been asked by other students concerning group counseling which may be helpful in explaining how you will fit in group counseling. You may have other questions or thoughts to discuss so please feel free to ask your counselor.

What Is Group Counseling?

Group counseling can mean many things to many people, but it provides an opportunity to:

1. talk about common concerns or problems
2. express your feelings in a small group
3. help you to understand how you are seen by others

How Often Do We Meet?

The group will meet at least one period a week for a number of weeks that your counselor has suggested. Meetings will begin on time and end on time.

Who Is Going To Be in the Group?

We will have at least one counselor and 5 to 10 other students who have expressed an interest in discussing their feelings, goals, and other interests. The group members may be all girls, all boys or sometimes both. Very seldom are more than two grade levels represented.

What Can I Gain by Being in a Group?

1. You may come to understand others in the group more clearly.
2. This understanding of others can help you to see and evaluate yourself more clearly.

Group Leadership

3. You may gain an understanding of your strengths and benefit from these.
4. It gives you a place to express yourself and your feelings.
5. You may find you have concerns similar to others in the group and realize that you are not alone.

What Will Be Expected of Me?

Some of the things the group would expect of you would be:
1. to be there on time
2. to be honest
3. be willing to listen to the others
4. be willing to respond to others

Do I Have To Be in the Group?

No, but we would like you to be if you want to.

Can I Quit the Group?

You may leave the group anytime you wish to do so.

Would You Like to Reserve a Place?

Your Objectives:

Thanks is given to Al Finlayson, Counselor, Orange Unified School District, Orange, California, for his permission to use this pamphlet. Readers have permission to reproduce the pamphlet to distribute to their students.

Author's Note: To be used as an inductive tool with adults.

APPENDIX F

OPEN LETTER: AN INDUCTION TOOL
FOR ADULTS

A OPEN LETTER

To: A Fellow Group Member
From: A Co-member
Re: Open Letter

Dear _____:

I just found out that we are going to be in group together and I am delighted that I will have the opportunity to interact with you. Since we will be traveling unknown territory, I would like to share with you some of the thoughts I have concerning this experience. If you are like me, you are not quite sure of the rules. I know something is expected of us. I most certainly expect to get something out of it or I wouldn't have joined—but just what is rather unclear at this point. I would guess that you share some of the anxieties which I am experiencing and might be interested in my thoughts as I approach this new, rather frightening experience.

First of all, I am wondering what it's going to be like—this being called "group." I have heard some bad things about groups—tales of people being stripped of their defenses and left there, tales of super-emotional binges which left people wondering what happened the next day, descriptions of personal privacy being probed in a way that amounted to psychological voyeurism. I am sure that you, as I, have heard of groups where members and leaders seemed to gain what amounted to masochistic-sadistic "kicks" watching individual members being torn to shreds in the name of the "new honesty" and "gut-level sensitivity." I would not care to experience all these things, and as protection I very carefully selected a leader who, because of his competency and theoretical orientation, had control of the group process and could block destructive elements.

I believe that group *can* be a very good thing—exciting, stimulating, joyous, and growth-motivating. I expect to gain some very specific things from the interaction. I hope for one thing that I will become less defensive and learn to know and express my feelings more accurately. I also hope I can release more self-actualizing forces within me and maybe even give up manipulative behaviors altogether. I most certainly want to increase my ability to establish and maintain tax-free relationships. I hope I will learn to express more freely a caring for others and perhaps even come to care more for *me*. I do look forward to being able to experience encounters more frequently, and maybe I will

259

even be able to develop that intuitiveness which I have observed in others who have been in groups for sensing open, nondefensive people. I would wish that my sense of alienation would diminish and that my spontaneity in responding to others would increase. I hope that my hunger for resonance will be met, as you and others in our group share how it is with you with me. In very simple terms, I guess I see group as a source of human nourishment to me.

I am aware that I cannot depend only on the group leader or other members to make the group experience a positive one. I am keenly conscious of the responsibilities I carry now that I have committed myself to group membership. First of all, I see myself as contracting with all of you to participate in the interaction. I know that inevitably I will *react,* but I also know that I must *interact.* Just as I hope to obtain resonance from you, so will I expect to provide you with feedback on how I am experiencing you. I know that I am the only one who can tell you how it is with me—how I am reacting to you. If I withhold this information from you, I am not meeting my obligations to you as a fellow group member. I will probably want to hide behind silence at times, and I know it will take courage on my part to take the risk of telling you how I am reacting to you. You may reject me whether my reactions are positive or negative, and the thought of this makes me anxious. I am very conscious of my inadequacies in transmitting accurately my emotions and thoughts and I hope that you will be patient with me as I struggle to communicate. I also hope that you and all of the group members will remember that I never really am talking about you, no matter what I say, but always about me. In turn, I know that the reverse is true—that, as you react to me, you really are making statements about you—never about me. If I choose to internalize your observations because they seem useful and accurate, I can do so, but I do not want to experience being judged by you or to experience judging you. This would diminish both of us, whether we are judge or judger.

As a group member, I perceive that I have entered into other obligations. For example, I agree that what occurs in our group remains there. I do not expect to transmit to another, no matter how close he is, what happens in our group. This belongs to us and only to us. I also realize that I have an obligation to attend all meetings if I possibly can. I am very aware that my absence sends a message that I had a choice to make and that my priority was not our group.

As I experience group with you, I hope that I do not intrude into your private life space. I also reserve on my part the right to introduce into the group only those things I choose from my life outside the group. As we interact, there will be so much going on "here and now" that most of our "there and then" experiences will intrude. I would rather we expended our time and energies on responding to each other, to really listen, and hear *meanings,* not just words. I also will try to be sensitive to your non-verbal communications, to respond to your body language and your voice intonations, as well as your spoken words. I hope that I can be open and authentic and share my feelings, thoughts, and experiencings with you, rather than relate to you as an object. I want you to experience me as there and available—a subject to be communicated with, not an object to be dissected.

I do not expect that our journey together will always be comfortable. As we encounter each other, we may have moments of confrontation which involve hostility, but I hope that I do not deny to you expression of those feelings, nor you to me, though neither of us may be pleased with them. I want you to accept and understand my conflicts, just as I hope that I can accept and understand yours. I would wish that you really try to help me solve problems I may choose to bring to the group, and that I can do the same for you. If, however, you find me giving advice or interceding in your efforts to face a situation fully, I hope you will point this out. I am sure that as you provide feedback to me—I-to-Thou —I will come to understand myself better and will gain in knowledge of myself. I will try to express honest warmth and acceptance if I feel this way and I hope that, if you feel these things, you will express them to me. I hope the group will become empathic as we share ourselves. If I experience too much coldness, or noncaring, or indifference, I think I will leave. This would diminish me and I do not choose to be diminished by the group process. I do choose to try to communicate as fully as possible, to give and receive confrontation, and to give and receive encounters. I am certain that there *is* life after birth and I believe that group is one way to find it. I would like to try.

Sincerely,

INDEX